then & now

The changing face of Plymouth

written & compiled by

Chris Robinson

edited by

Ben Robinson

Pen&ink
PUBLISHING

British Library Cataloguing in Publication Data
Robinson Chris 1954 –
Plymouth Then & Now, photographic comparisons 1860s - 2006
1.Devon. Plymouth, history
1. Title
942.3'58

ISBN 0 9543 4804 4

Designed By Chris Robinson
Cover design by Ewan McKnight
Edited by Ben Robinson
© Chris Robinson 2006

First published November 2006

OTHER CHRIS ROBINSON TITLES
PUBLISHED BY PEN & INK

PLYMOUTH AS TIME DRAWS ON – 1985
PLYMOUTH AS TIME DRAWS ON VOL 2 – 1988
VICTORIAN PLYMOUTH: AS TIME DRAWS ON – 1991
PUBS OF PLYMOUTH PAST AND PRESENT
The Harvest Home and one hundred others – 1995
PUBS OF PLYMOUTH PAST AND PRESENT
Prince George and one hundred others – 1997
UNION STREET – 2000
THE ARGYLE BOOK – 2002
ELIZABETHAN PLYMOUTH – 2002
PLYMOUTH THEN & NOW – 2004
IT CAME TO OUR DOOR [revised] – 2005
PLYMOUTH COLLEGE: The First Hundred Years – 2005

Published by
Pen & Ink Publishing
34 New Street
Barbican
Plymouth PL1 2NA
tel; 01752 705337/228120
fax; 01752 770001
www.chrisrobinson.co.uk

Printed & bound in Great Britain by
Latimer Trend & Company Ltd
Estover Close
Plymouth PL6 7PL
Devon

then & now

then & now

The changing face of Plymouth

Introduction

On 7 November 2004 I took the last image to be included in the first volume of Plymouth Then & Now; it depicted early work in the foundation laying of the new Drake Circus complex. Now that work is finished – the biggest undertaking since the first phase of reconstruction after the war. It is the third Drake Circus to have been built on this site in the last hundred years. It is also the biggest, and its impact on the City Centre is inevitably going to be enormous as it is the first structure you see coming in on two of the four main approaches into to the heart of the city's retail operations.

As far as the façade is concerned the local jury has been divided over the building's aesthetic impact but even the most skeptical are looking forward to exploring the insides before they finally make up their minds. Meanwhile all around the fringes of the low-slung, post-war shopping centre there have been other major developments – around Sutton Harbour, the University, Exeter Street, the Crescent and Derry's Cross … and there are many more developments planned; indeed just weeks before Drake Circus was completed, news was announced of major new developments for the West End of the City Centre (around Western Approach and Colin Campbell Court), and for Millbay. What state will they be in two years from now? And what of the proposed 24-storey skyscraper mooted for the YMCA site at the corner of Armada Way and Cobourg Street, or the 25-storey tower in front of Drake Circus? Maybe in a few years time there will be many more new vistas and vantage points to consider. For the time being however let us look back over the last few years.

As with the previous volume the various picture pairings have all appeared at some time or another in the Western Evening Herald and each little feature includes the date of that first publication. In some instances life has moved on again and even one or two of the Now pictures may appear dated – but that's really the point … nothing stays the same forever, and it's fun to plot and spot the changes.

And while the characteristic feature of those changes in the heart of the city is undoubtedly a dramatic increase in building heights, there can be little doubt, in this fast growing city, that, away from the centre,

ROWE STREET Scheduled to be in use from 2007 the University's Rowe Street development (which will incorporate elements of the Faculty of Arts), sits directly opposite the new Drake Circus car park and shopping mall; it is one of a great many sites that the University have redeveloped in the last decade or so and all the indications are that there are more proposals in the pipeline. The impact of this expanding academic instituion on the regeneration of the city, particularly around North Hill and Mutley Plain has been enormous; culturally, economically and socially and anyone revisiting the city after an absence of ten years or more can't fail to notice the the increasing numbers of students and student friendly venues. *EH 7 Oct 2006*

the development is about to be marked by an even more dramatic decrease in the number of green fields within our expanding civic waistline. Vast swathes of grassland have fallen recently to developers at Derriford, Plympton and Plymstock, but the counter will soon go off the scale as the new town at Sherford, just south of the A38, takes shape. Those areas barely feature in this volume, but plans are afoot to chronicle life east of the Plym in the next volume of Then & Now.

In the meantime, make yourself comfortable and prepare to spend a happy hour or so flicking through this collection; I have little doubt that you'll quickly lose count of the number of times you think to yourself, 'oh yes, I'd forgotten that', or 'was it really that long ago', or 'blimey, I didn't know that had gone!'

Chris Robinson
October 2006

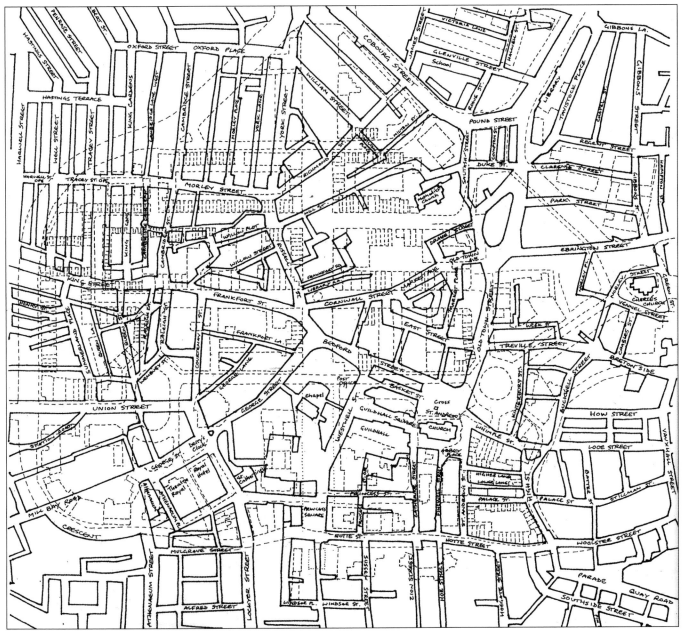

Having spent many hours over the years trying to work out what was where in terms of the pre and post-war city centre I decided to draw up this pair of overlaid maps highlighting, in the one version, the old street pattern and in the other, the modern street arrangement. I used them both for the first time in Victorian Plymouth and again in the previous volume of Then & Now; and I make no apology for including them here again. They are as useful to me now as they have always been and so I have little doubt that others too will find them helpful, not just in the context of this book, but generally when looking at any old images of the heart of Plymouth.

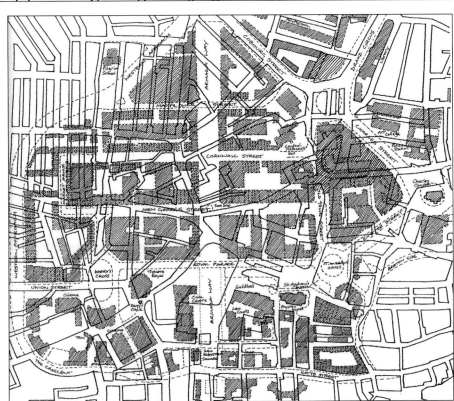

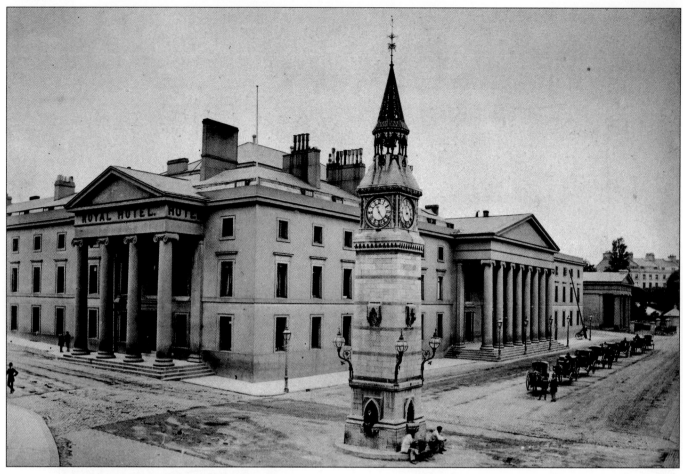

ACKNOWLEDGEMENTS

Over the years that I have been taking these Then & Now pairings I have been regularly surprised and delighted to find odd offerings in my Herald mailbag from readers who have taken the time and trouble to put their own 'shots from the same spot' together. I hope I have managed to recall them all, if I've forgotten anyone, please accept my sincere apologies. Similarly if you see a photograph here that you know is yours and yet you have not been credited or consulted, again, I apologise. With so many images coming from so many sources – and with so little information, if anything at all, recorded on the back of them, it is difficult to be as thorough as one would like to be. So thanks to the Herald Library, Plymouth Central Library, Plymouth City Art Gallery and Museum. However the publishers would be happy to hear from anyone who has information concerning the copyright of any uncredited images.

Certainly I know the source of almost all of the Now images, for I took them myself, and for anyone who has never tried to make their own Then & Now pairings, I can heartily recommend the practice. It's always a pleasant challenge to try and find that exact spot that the previous photographer occupied and it can be an odd sensation when you do think you've found that spot … you often wonder what the original photographer would have made of the same view today.

There are actually one or two instances in these pages where I have taken both shots … and all being well, there will doubtless be more of them in the future – after all I've been drawing and photographing Plymouth for over thirty years now – however that doesn't make the process any less odd, in fact there can be quite a sense of loss if the original subject of a photo has disappeared altogether, especially if you cherished happy memories of that place. The Drake Cinema is a good case in point. Drake Circus - seventies-style - not so good, but even there it's hard to believe that it only now exists in the mind and in photographs and other archive footage.

And that's an opportune moment to thank all those others who have been recording aspects of the Changing Face of Plymouth, whether for fun, financial gain or for posterity. So thank you; Roy Westlake, Roy Todd, Peter Carlyle, Robin Blythe-Lord, Peter Waterhouse, Anne Tolley, Keith George, Bob Cook, Graham Langstone, Vincent Hart, Thelma Malthouse, Trevor Lear and George Williams. Thanks too to Herald photographers Pete Holgate, Mike Cox, Guy Channing, Tony Carney and many others past and present, similarly to the various editors of the paper I've worked with over the last twenty-five years, most notably in recent years; Alan Cooper; Rachel Campey; Alan Qualtrough and Bill Martin.

Thanks to the ever-patient features team at the paper; Mike Bramhall, Martin Freeman, Su Carroll, Jackie Butler and Cherie Gordon … and to Carol Saunders and Steve Grant. And the even more patient, and long-suffering, Rob Warren and Doreen Mole - the Plymouth Prints team at New Street. To wife and publisher, Clare; to son and editor, Ben, to parent and outlaws, Des, Trish and Pops for support and proof reading. And to the rest of the family and friends just for being there.

Contents

then & now

The changing face of Plymouth

written & compiled by
Chris Robinson

AERIAL CITY CENTRE (*next page*) Woolworths was almost complete, Dingles had just begun. Royal Parade had been laid out, Armada Way was in its infancy. The Prudential building was still standing, as was the Corn Exchange and the twenty-year-old Odeon cinema. Our Then picture takes us back to 21 September 1949 and can be seen more fully in the recently revised Pat Twyford book It Came To Our Door. It was taken by then Herald photographer Dermot Fitzgerald, while our Now image was taken by the Herald's current picture editor, Pete Holdgate, this year, 2005, and it can be seen more fully - and in colour - in the Herald's new Eye in the Sky supplement - both publications available from the Herald shop in Armada Way. While sometimes it is a challenge to find the same vantage point for terrestrial pictures it is quite remarkable how these two Herald men virtually found the same spot in the air! *EH 03 Dec 2005*

THE BELVEDERE Then you don't see it, Now you do ... the colonnaded Belvedere that when first erected sat above the imposing entrance to the Promenade Pier. What is particularly fascinating about this Then picture is that while the Belvedere hasn't yet been put in place, Smeaton's Tower has. This tells us therefore that our older image dates from somewhere between 1884, when the removal of Smeaton's Tower from the Eddystone Reef to the Hoe had been completed, and 1891, when work began on the creation of the Belvedere. Incidentally prior to that time, the flat area on the landward side of the road, set back from the pier head, was known as the Bull Ring and here it was that many a major meeting was held, with thousands congregating in this mini amphitheatre to hear a speaker in the days before amplification was available. *EH 22 Oct 2005*

BULL RING The laying out of the Hoe Park as a cultivated parkland to be enjoyed by the people of the Three Towns had only just begun when this photograph was taken by W Heath in (or before) 1890. Elliot Terrace, the Esplanade, the Grand Hotel and the Royal Western Yacht Club alongside it, were all relatively new (the Grand had been open barely ten years), hence their novelty value to the pioneering Plymouth photographer. Perhaps Mr Heath was also aware that this view was about to change yet again with the construction of the colonnaded Belvedere - on the site of the old Bull Ring - in the middle distance where the two men are seated in a small shelter (the Corporation Seat erected in 1832 and incorporated into the Belvedere in 1891). *EH 09 Dec 2006*

HOE PIER Plymouth Pier, as anyone alive will remember it, did not look like this, for it should have a large, domed pavilion on the end of it; but that 2,000 seater facility was not erected on the end of the pier until 1891, a year or so after this photograph was taken. The Pier, as we see it here, was opened in May 1884. It had always been the original intention to build the pavilion (and to create the pier entrance above the Bull Ring – where the Belevedere now stands), but there was a funding problem and the pier was sold in 1887. It was the new owners who completed the pavilion. Fifty years later however, during the Blitz of 1941, the timber-floored pier was reduced to a metal skeleton by enemy incendiaries and the pier was never rebuilt. *EH 18 Nov 2006*

TINSIDE AND DRAKE'S ISLAND Take away the people and possibly the warship and you'd be hard pressed to spot too many changes in this pair of pictures. Mount Edgcumbe Country Park has changed little over the last 200 years, let alone the last fifty, while Drake's Island, which could have – and perhaps, should have – changed, looks, from this distance at least, much as it has always done. Perhaps the most discernable difference is to be found within the parameters of the pool itself as one of the victims of the recent, and very welcome, refurbishment of the Tinside Lido was the removal of the little diving board on the seaward side. Otherwise let's hope that it's pretty much business as usual in another fifty years time. *EH 18 Mar 2006*

MOUNT BATTEN FROM THE HOE The Royal Plymouth Corinthian Yacht Club has been a constant fixture on the Hoe frontage for over a hundred years – but there's no sign of it in our Then picture. As we stand on the well-beaten, earthen track above the Lion's Den at East Hoe the similarities between our two images are more immediate than the differences but there are plenty. Taken in the late 1880s our early image pre-dates the Corinthian's arrival here by almost ten years. It is also strange to reflect that for most of that intervening period (at least seventy-five years) Mountbatten was used as an RAF base, however there was little thought of aeroplanes back Then and, apart from a handful of converted buildings, there is little evidence of it today. Note the ever-present seventeenth century tower on the top of the headland and the then new Breakwater Inn at the end of the Mountbatten pier. *EH 11 Nov 2006*

FISHER'S NOSE Older Plymothians may just be able to remember when the only coastal route around to the Hoe from the Barbican was via a narrow tunnel like affair popularly known as "the Cage Walk". It was an arrangement that lasted until the mid-1930s when eventually the decision was taken to properly join the relatively new road in front of the Citadel – Madeira Road - with the more established Commercial Road at the back of the former victualling buildings (one or two of which them later become biscuit factories, and almost all of which are now gone). Previously the spur from this south-eastern corner of the seventeenth century Citadel had run down to Fisher's Nose and it served as a means for getting troops and supplies in and out of the massive fortification, by boat, within minimum risk of attack or observation. Now the seaward side is occupied by Duttons Cafe, providing victuals cooked on the premises for locals and tourists alike. *EH 30 July 05*

HOE BOWLING CLUB More than half a century separates the two images and apart from being taken at different times of the year, the similarities are far more striking than the differences. There are quite a few though, as, from the left, we see that the big trees have gone (but they have been replaced), Smeaton's Tower has had its stripes restored and a natural windbreak (the shape of a long hedge) has appeared to shelter the bowlers from the sea breezes. Close inspection reveals that the fencing has changed slightly but not too much and certainly not enough to affect the enjoyment of passing spectators who like the idea that bowls is still being played somewhere on the Hoe more than four hundred years after Sir Francis Drake played his famous game near here. *EH 11 Mar 2006*

PHOENIX WHARF 16 February 1905 is the date our Then picture postcard was sent from Plymouth to Falmouth. Remarkably despite the passage of 100 years the foreground of this setting is little changed today. The building on the right (currently operating as the Mayflower Sailing Club) is the sole survivor of the great complex of buildings that once lined the waterfront here, but from this angle there is no indication of those particular changes. Across the other side of the water the waterline and the skyline have changed enormously; the Queen Anne Battery Marina and Royal Western Yacht Club appearing here in the 1980s, the changes in the background taking place over a longer period of time. For all that, however, it is interesting to note that the appetite for trips on pleasure boats is seemingly every bit as healthy as it was then. *EH 20 Aug 2005*

COMMERCIAL WHARF Just to the side of the so-called Mayflower Steps are another set of steps even closer to the original location of the stone stairway purportedly used by the Pilgrims. Some seventy-something years ago this particular portal stood within the shelter of the old Barbican Watch House, for many years the home station of the local Police force, as indeed it was when our Then photo (kindly supplied by Bob Cook) was taken. In those days Commercial Road still had a substantial commercial element to it – these were the old victualling yard premises created before the Stonehouse Victualling Yard was built and replete with baking and brewing facilities. In later years home to biscuit manufactories and emigration facilities, they also came to serve as residential dwellings. Today only one major building survives from that time – the Mayflower Sailing Club, standing in splendid isolation alongside Phoenix Wharf. *EH 10 Jun 2006*

WEST PIER Notwithstanding the changes taking place in and around Drake Circus, one of the most radically altered vistas in the City over the last ten years has to be that along the whole eastern waterfront of Sutton Harbour. Long gone now are the coal yards, the motley collection of two or three storey sheds and warehouses, and the gap between the piers that rendered the harbour tidal. Now in their place we have the relocated Fish Market, the National Marine Aquarium, offices, hotels and residential accommodation, some of it on reclaimed land, and with each successive development seemingly higher than the last. Then, of course, there are the lock gates and the ever-encroaching pontoons stretching out across the water itself, giving the area an ever-increasing Mediterranean feel. *EH 03 Jun 2006*

FISH MARKET This fascinating study from the late nineteenth century shows us just what fish trading was like on the Barbican prior to the widening of the quay and the construction, in the mid-late 1890s, of the new Fish Market. Over 110 years later and that Fish Market has, itself, been superseded and the building is now put to other, less messy, commercial uses. In those days, as we see here quite graphically, the landward transport used was horse-drawn or hand carts, and men and women, whatever their status, wore hats. Note too the Railways and Parcel Office on the left – this was for material that travelled across the seas on Great Western Steamers. Today the building still stands, and some of that old writing is preserved, but the buildings beyond, between it and the Island House (Then out of view) are long-gone, victims of the Blitz. *EH 01 Oct 2005*

BARBICAN WATCH HOUSE Having recently re-examined this wonderful early Barbican image it seemed like a good time to revisit the approximate spot that our Victorian photographer would have stopped at over 115 years ago. The key here is the quay - soon after this picture was taken what is now the old fish market was built on land reclaimed from Sutton Pool. The original harbour line is still visible today (where the pattern of the cobbles alters). Perhaps the biggest change here though is towards the end of the Barbican; in our Then picture we see the old Watch House and a surviving early Victualling Building where now we have open space and the beginning of the road that runs around the eastern and southern slopes of the Citadel. With all the work currently being undertaken elsewhere around the harbour today, one can but wonder if one day there will not, once more, be buildings on this site opposite the Admiral MacBride. *EH 26 Feb 2005*

THE BARBICAN A load of bollards – that's the principal visual difference between these two images taken some forty years apart. The bollards define the boundary between city land and Sutton Harbour land on the seaward side which is what was reclaimed from the harbourside to build the original fish market in the 1890s. Back in the 1960s AH Moody & Son were operating a Yacht Brokerage out of what is now, and has long been Platters, Charles Cload still had his Ship and Yacht Chandler's store alongside it and the ever-present Dolphin, had an empty site alongside it (the site became part of the pub in an extension effected over twenty years ago). On the other side of the road, the Navy has experienced a few cosmetic changes but is substantially the same, as are the other buildings that constitute this corner of the Barbican. *EH 18 Feb 2006*

FISH MARKET Two fishermen pass the time of day in a time when the fish market was just behind them. Part of the then new offices, and ice house are visible to our left in the Then picture while in our Now image we see the brand new pontoon, designed to cater for a completely different market, to our right. The Fish Market is now on the other side of the harbour and whereas there were no leisure pontoons in Sutton Pool over thirty years ago, today the demands of the yachting industry have led to the creation of hundreds of floating moorings. The changes on water reflect, quite literally, changes on the waterfront, as new high-rise apartment blocks increasingly come to dominate the quaysides. *EH 04 Feb 2006*

CUSTOMS HOUSE On the face of it there appears to be little more than cosmetic change here; the Three Crowns has undergone a major facelift, the Customs House looks much the same and the buildings to the left of it, as we look at it here, are have lost a chimney or two but apparently little else. The real clue to the passing of more than forty years comes from the cranes on the skyline as we see that the topping out of the Civic Centre has not quite been completed and over to the far left we see the bottom of High Street (now known as Buckwell Street) before it was demolished to make way for the 'new' flats that stand there today. Note too the changing design of the street lighting. *EH 11 Feb 2006*

QUAY ROAD The similarities are perhaps more striking than you would expect given the changes that have taken place around the fringes of Sutton Harbour over the last ten to twenty years. Our Then picture takes us back to the first decade of the twentieth century, when petrol-driven two-wheeled transport was extremely rare and horse-drawn or hand-drawn carts were the most favoured form of land transport and, of course, all fishing boats would have relied on sail power. Note also the strength and length of the shadows, indicating fairly strong summer sunlight, and yet everyone in the photograph is wearing a jacket or thick jumper and, without exception, a hat or cap. The Fish Market was relatively newly-built back then, now it has moved to the other side of the Harbour and the Edinburgh Woollen Mill has just taken on the old market premises – until recently occupied by Dartington Glass. *EH 25 June 2005*

PLYMOUTH, THE BARBICAN.

SUTTON HARBOUR On the skyline the distinctive features of Sutton High School can be seen looking back across Sutton Harbour. However the building is no longer a school and the character of the Harbour it looks out on has changed enormously too. Most of the warehousing has gone or been converted and bold new housing developments dominate the waterfront. From this perspective though perhaps the biggest change is the entrance to the harbour, now controlled by lock gates. *EH 09 Oct 2004*

SUTTON HARBOUR The skyline holds the key, for despite the fact that these two images aren't quite taken from the same quay, the silhouettes of St Andrew's Church tower and the Guildhall tower tells that the angle is much the same. In our Then image we find ourselves standing on the far side of the harbour at the entrance to what was, before the recent infilling, Coxside Creek (now Lockyer's Quay), the harbour was clearly tidal and seemingly a happy place to swim and play judging by the boys we can see in the water and the muddy foreground. By contrast with 'Now' all of the boats 'Then', rather than just some of them, were working boats and while today you may not see many swimming for fun in the harbour, most of the boats here now are leisure and pleasure based. Thanks, incidentally, to Bob Cook for this wonderful Victorian image of Sutton Harbour. *EH 01 Jul 2006*

SUTTON POOL Thanks to David King for this fascinating pair of images. It all seems so familiar but so much has changed. We travel back to the early 1970s for our Then image; Sutton Harbour was still tidal, the sea ebbing and flowing through East and West Pier, the Fish Market was at the end of Quay Road, and there were coal wharves at Coxside. In the intervening years, yachts have become more commonplace than fishing boats; jetties and marinas have stretched out over the water; a new Fish Market has been built on reclaimed land at Coxside and new Lock Gates ensure that all parts of the Sutton Pool are accessible at all states of the tide. Meanwhile on the other side of the gates, Queen Anne's Battery is now a major yachting centre and further across our view, the former RAF Mountbatten site now is too. What changes will the future unfold? Hopefully, whatever they are, with so much accommodation being created around the fringes of the pool to take advantage of the water-filled vistas, they won't involve losing any more of the waterfront. *EH 28 May 2005*

SUTTON HARBOUR Before you ask which one is Then and which is Now have another look. Admittedly not a lot of time has passed between the taking of the two aerial images (the Now appearing in the current Herald 'Eye in the Sky' supplement), but a great deal has happened; for one thing, the tide is right out in our Then picture and that's something you don't see now that the lock gates are in place, so it suggests a good ten year time lapse. But not much more as the China House had already been redeveloped and the transformation of North Quay was already well under way – but plenty has happened there since Then as you can see. And with the Fish Quay still on the western side of Sutton Harbour, there was still parking and an additional building in Quay Road. You can also see that there's a little more mooring available now for those who park in the water! Big changes in Bretonside and Exeter Street too. *EH 17 Dec 2005*

HOW STREET Fifty or so years ago when our Then picture showing a vintage car rally at the top of How Street was taken, the car we see most prominently was the best part of fifty years old itself. Look now at our Now picture and although it's not a particularly comforting thought, there is every chance that, another hundred years from now, the cars we see here in the Nat West Bank car park will look as quaint and curious as the old beauty in our Then picture. Perhaps the car will have been superseded by another mode of transport altogether, who knows? Looking beyond the cars we can see that apart from a face-lift, the flats in How Street look much the same, as does the shop on the corner, only then it was a dairy and now, it is a hairdressers' – and indeed has been for many years. *EH 30 April 2005*

NOTTE STREET The street is wider, some of the buildings a little higher. The cobbles are covered and the hand cart is a thing of the past. This is Notte Street, two images separated by over sixty years and not a building left to anchor our impression. The topography is little changed, however the street line is much the same and one can only wonder what someone from 1937 brought straight into 2004 would make of it all. *EH 23 Oct 2004*

ST ANDREW STREET In order to try and duplicate the look of the Then picture we've come a little further down St Andrew Street, consequently the pub on the right of the Then shot is what was the Abbey Hotel (and is now Kitty O'Hanlons), while the pub on the right in the Now picture was the White Swan in 1937 (and a little further down the street) and is now Bigwigs. The end of St Andrew's Church is clearly visible Then and remained so until the 1970s when the Magistrate's Court was built. A little hazy, but also discernable, in the Then picture is Spooner's Corner at the bottom of Old Town Street. Note also the Farley's Rusks lorry and the old ice factory on the right. *EH 12 Feb 2005*

ELIM CHURCH Built by Isaac Foot senior in the 1880s, in front of the old Mayoralty House in Notte Street (and one time home of William Cookworthy), the old Mission Hall building was gutted by enemy bombing during the Second World War. Subsequently sold, for a nominal sum, by David Nash (a grandson of Isaac Foot) to the Elim Church (whose Congregation had been worshipping in Stonehouse), the building continued to serve in an ecclesiastical role until 1983 when the congregation moved on again, this time to Embankment Road. The building here was then transformed into a restaurant by Michael and Jill Robinson, who rechristened the place, the Barbican Revival. Now, after the passing of another twenty years or so, it is known as Arribas – a Mexican style restaurant complete with lively new signage and wooden shutters. *EH 09 Sep 2006*

JUBILEE HOTEL Drivers won a few feet of roadway and drinkers lost two notable old pubs – the Jubilee at the eastern entrance to Sutton Road, and the Burton Boys on the western corner. Many were the protests and all of them in vain. It was twenty-five years ago that these two licensed premises were sacrificed and the road was reconfigured, but, apart from that, the changes here have been relatively small, it is only when you turn around and face the other way that Exeter Street starts to look very different. Indeed one can but wonder how soon it will be before development in the area we see here starts going up and up with many of the existing low buildings being demolished. Curiously enough, however, the erstwhile Lower Street Mission building on the right is probably safe for a good while yet. *EH 21 Jul 2006*

BURTON BOYS Today the former Lower Street Mission Hall, no longer obscured by the old Burton Boys pub, stands clear in the middle ground of this view. In the foreground the Autocare brand has replaced that of Autofactors, a car concern that has been established here many years now, otherwise there have been a few incidental changes to the road markings and layout, but it is in the backdrop that the changes have been truly staggering. Gradually the building line has climbed higher and higher, mainly over the last decade or so, and as it has done so, one would guess that the life expectancy of many of the single-storey developments in the immediate area has gone down and down. *EH 05 Aug 2006*

ST LUKE'S While the view looking up Tavistock Place hasn't changed all that greatly in the past 50 years, if you were to have been leaning on that lamppost looking south when our Then picture was taken, you would have seen a vastly different vista. No Art College then at the end of Regent Street, as the short kink in the road led us down towards Drake Circus. Back then, St Luke's was still a church, indeed, after the destruction of Charles Church, this was, for a time in the 1950s and early 1960s, the parish church (of Charles with St Luke). Then it was superceded by a new arrangement with St Matthias, and the library services took over the erstwhile ecclesiastical building. In this currently student-dominated environment the neighbouring properties have found favour as cafes. *EH 18 Jan 2003*

CHARLES STREET Charles Street ... Now you see it ... Then, you didn't – not quite anyway. From the Herald archive comes this fascinating mid-sixties shot showing us just where Charles Street would run. At that time Ebrington Street still ran in a continuous line from the eastern section that survives today, right through to Old Town Street On the corner of Ebrington Street and Norley Place, the Norley Inn was still standing, as indeed were both the Revenue (roughly in the middle of our Then picture) and the late-lamented Harvest Home - seen here just to the left of the building that now houses the Roundabout pub. The latter building is one of two common elements, the other is the former Public Secondary School premises, the roof of which is just discernable either side of the Revenue. *EH 24 Sep 2005*

CHARLES CHURCH *(Left)*

Seldom has a Then and Now pairing in this series been separated by so few years. It was in 1999 that the middle view of the seventeenth century Charles Church was taken, and while the fabric of that ancient structure looks much as it has done since it was burnt out during the last war, all around it there are signs of change. Traffic lights now control the flow of vehicles onto the roundabout and allow for easier pedestrian access around it; while on the other side the 1970s car park is no more and the most iconic part of the new Drake Circus shopping complex frames the church … to the approval of some and the chagrin of others. *EH 23 Sep 2006*

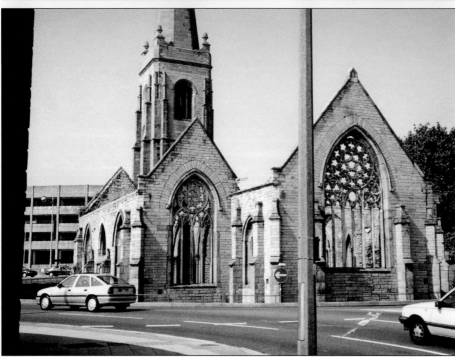

CHARLES STREET *(Right)* The

angle on the most recent shot is not quite right, however Charles Street is busier with traffic now than it has ever been and the new road layout means that the original vantage point is currently in the middle of the nearside traffic lane and yours truly didn't fancy standing in the road with his back to the oncoming vehicles - especially right outside the police station. The main focal point however is the tower of Charles Church with the Staddon Heights skyline behind it and there is little change there. To our left the steps up from Charles Street to the Art College entrance give us another bearing, on the right however everything has changed. Gone is the car park and the 'old' Drake Circus (which was still a few years off when our top shot taken in 1964) and in its place the massive new indoor shopping mall and car park that is the new Drake Circus. Originally designed with one finish along Charles Street, the local authority later requested three distinct facades (indeed they had wanted three separate structures) and what you see is the comprimise solution. *EH 04 Nov 2006*

EXETER STREET The road pattern is the same and Charles Church looks exactly as it has done for more than sixty years now, and yet although not a huge time differential separates these two images there are changes almost everywhere else you look. The street furniture is new, the bottom back end of the new Drake Circus shopping complex is very new, on the far right, the Staples building is fairly new and in between there are a number of developments that have popped up over the last two decades, almost all of them rising higher than anything previously known in this part of town. Today our view of that familiar limestone pile that was Sutton High School for Boys is obscured by various residential and educational premises, many associated with the University, while our view out across the green tree tops of Beaumont Park is similarly being blocked by modern buildings. *EH 15 Jul 2006*

VIEW FROM BOOTS The key uniting these two images, separated by more than fifty years, is the building on the far left in both images. For those who aren't sure of the current vantage point, we're looking out of window of Boots' staircase, over looking the top end of New George Street, and straight into the entrance to the car park/access area behind Lloyds Bank in Plymouth City Centre. When Arthur Turner took his original photograph back in the early fifties he was a teenager working on the construction of Boots and, as you can see, the bank had yet to be built, St Andrew's Church was still in process of being reconstructed and part of the old market complex and the old Corn Exchange (on the right of Arthur's view) was still standing. *EH 16 Apr 2005*

FRANKFORT STREET Our Then picture (supplied by Pete Waterhouse) shows Frankfort Street as it appeared for the best part of ten years, after the 1941 Blitz and before the completion of Woolworths in 1950. The film Skylark (starring Ray Milland and Claudette Colbert and released in 1941), is showing at the Odeon, the cinema that was pulled down in 1963 and which stood where Littlewoods now is. The street line of New George Street is a little different to that of old Frankfort Street, consequently we can't quite achieve the same vantage point. However, the façade of the then new Leicester Harmsworth House (it was completed in 1938) provides a fine visual link between the two images. *EH 27 Nov 2004*

BOOTS Standing on this corner and looking straight across to Boots, you could be forgiven for thinking that, apart from surface cosmetics, little has changed in the last fifty years or so. Cast your gaze a little to the right and any time-traveller might raise an eyebrow. The pre-war Drake Circus complete with its late-1930s Guinness clock (which later went to Bristol), came down in the mid-1960s; the next Drake Circus went up almost a decade later, and came down thirty years after that. Now we have the newly-opened, 2006 Drake Circus – bigger and closer than ever. Is there a time-traveller out there who can tell us what we will see from here in another thirty years? *EH 25 Nov 2006*

POPHAMS Travelling back over fifty years here we find a Royal Parade without Spooners, Yeos or Pophams. Within a few years however they would all be in place and today, of course, all of them still stand, but those names have gone, with Debenhams accounting for the greater part of the change and Lloyds Bank now occupying most of what was Pophams. What is perhaps the most intriguing aspect of Arthur Turner's Then picture though is not so much what we can't yet see in it, but what we can, as this splendid moment in time offers us a fine view of the side elevation of Dingles, revealing just what marvellous piece of period architecture the building is from all angles, not just its more public frontages. *EH 04 Jun 2005*

OLD TOWN STREET With so many changes taking place at the top end of Old Town Street, it is perhaps remarkable that so little has changed in the last forty years at the bottom end. Clearly worlds apart from the pre-war view one would have had from here, the contemporary angle on this delightful Roy Westlake snap shows mainly cosmetic alterations on the southern side of St Andrew's Cross. Gone are the distinctive Belisha Beacons as street furniture and other artistic embellishments vie with the growing trees and advances in car design for the most obvious differences to spot. *EH 10 Sep 2005*

SPOONER'S CORNER There's nothing really concrete to link these two images – however the vantage point is virtually the same as we stand alongside the road crossing at what was Then and still is Now, the south-western corner of Old Town Street. Back Then in 1937 this was Spooner's Corner, today it is on the edge of St Andrew's Cross Roundabout. Then, as Now, this was one of the city's busiest junctions and buses still readily fill the frame for any photographer standing by. However these days, with more cars on the road, single-decker buses are more common than the old, much-loved double-deckers, with their hop-on-and-off rear access. *EH 15 Oct 2005*

ST ANDREW STREET The location of this wonderful image of pre-war Plymouth is clear enough when you compare it to its little-changed contemporary counterpart, but, in isolation, the people and the vehicles distract you from the common elements. We are, of course, standing outside the Magistrates Court in St Andrew Street, looking up towards the building we currently know as the Café Rouge – with the eastern end of St Andrew's to our left. Beyond the junction with Whimple Street clearly all has changed, as indeed it has behind us, but note otherwise how little altered is this quaint corner of old Plymouth. *EH 16 Dec 2006*

BRITISH HOME STORES Some thirty years on and British Home Stores has been rebranded – BHS - this section of Armada Way has been pedestrianised, and Hardy & Co have since been replaced by, first Courts, then Virgin. Otherwise it looks pretty much like business as usual here. Except that there is another change, like so many other City Centre department stores, BHS no longer sells food quite the way it used to. *EH 20 Nov 2004*

TOP SHOP Woolworth's was the first big store in Plymouth's post-war city centre. It started trading in 1950 and a year or two later Arthur Turner took this fascinating photograph of the development of what is now Top Shop and Top Man . It was originally opened as HA Leon & Co costumiers, with Manfield & Sons' shoe shop along from them (their signs are there on Coles' builders board) and then H Samuel the jewellers, note the clock is still there over fifty years on.. Running out of picture to the left as we stand here on Dingle's northwest corner, we see the end of King Street, the Barley Sheaf just out of view and the top of the old Odeon Cinema sticking up above the modern line of shops. *EH 23 Apr 2005*

SUN DIAL The best part of forty years separates these two images, and while a first glance of our Then picture will strike many in a very familiar way, it has been very different for almost twenty years now – since pedestrianisation removed the motor car from this section of Royal Parade and the sun dial arrived. Indeed a whole generation leaving school now will only know it as it is Now; although clearly there has been a significant change to the area to our immediate left here – as the space between Dingles and the Pearl Assurance Building was cleared at the end of last year. *EH 05 Nov 2005*

THE PIAZZA The backdrop hasn't altered much but what about the foreground? And here's another question – if you didn't know Plymouth at all, how easy do you think it would be to say which was the Then and which is the 'Now'? Remarkably everything in the foreground is changed, the trees are all new, the paving stones are all new and the street furniture and lighting is all new. The Now picture, complete with the BBC big screen and mobile Dewdney pasty van, was taken this week and the Then picture (sent in anonymously) was taken at least a couple of years ago and certainly after the Herald's move out to Derriford in the early-mid 1990s. *EH 08 Sep 2006*

THE UNDERPASS As I understand it the underpass constructed here in 1973 and opened that year just before Christmas is still there today, it's just that now it's not so much buried as filled in. Somehow it is difficult to escape the feeling that one day, doubtless in the lifetime of some who will remember it being built, it will be opened up again. For now though pedestrians can rejoice in a practical space that already has been put to good use as an open market venue, an ice-skating arena and an outdoor, big-screen, entertainment area. Meanwhile motorists scratch their heads and wonder. Incidentally, note how bland the underpass was until the jazzed-up tiles arrived a decade or so later. *EH 17 Sept 2005*

DINGLES Double-decker busses and a four-storey department store have been; in the first instance, largely replaced by single-decker busses; and, in the second instance, crowned with an additional (post-fire) two floors. Otherwise all appears here to be pretty much business as usual, even though more than fifty years have elapsed between the taking of the two images. What the pictures don't tell us however, is that in the intervening period a major pedestrian subway was created here, and that, after some thirty years' service, last year it was filled in so that the ground would once again be level at this location. Dingles opened for business, incidentally, in September 1951. *EH 14 May 2005*

PRUDENTIAL BUILDING There was a plaque on the old Prudential Building marking the fact that 'near this place formerly stood Frankfort Gate which formed, with others, the principal entrance to the town…"Prior to the construction of the Prudential at the beginning of the 20th Century, the plaque had, since 1813, been located on the wall of the Globe Theatre. This was pulled down in 1899. The gate, demolished in 1783, would have stood roughly in the middle of this view, almost in line with buildings on the other side of the City Square, here across from Dingles' Armada Way entrance. *EH 13 Nov 2004*

GUILDHALL AND POST OFFICE With the corner of St Andrew's Church tower just visible to the left, this is the scene that greeted the dawn on the morning of 21ˢᵗ March 1941. The dust is still settling and smoke is still rising from the ruins as servicemen, policemen and fire-fighters gather around apparently waiting for instructions. The Guildhall has been burnt out, so too has the wonderfully imposing Post Office in Westwell Street – seen here to the right of the tree in Guildhall Square. Out of picture, to our right, the Municipal Building had also been left a burnt-out shell, but of the much-photographed Victorian grouping, only the Guildhall would be rebuilt, and even then it would be several years after the war before that decision would be taken. *EH 26 Nov 2005*

WESTWELL STREET Opposite the Guildhall was the city's main Post Office, built in the late 19ᵗʰ century to replace an earlier one on the same site. Badly bomb-damaged during the last war, the Westwell Street site was cleared to become part of Armada Way. In our Now picture the dramatic Victorian building would have stood along the line of traffic bollards and streetlight. *EH 26 Oct 1998*

WESTERN APPROACH Clearly the layout of Western Approach here is much the same in both images, but where do we begin when it comes to highlighting the many differences between these two images, kindly supplied for us by Fred Guy? Starting from the left, the sign for 1600 Spaces tells us that Armada Centre and the Copthorne Hotel had not even been started and area above Mayflower Street, below North Cross, was still one big flat car park. Behind this sign we see that the block of flats has recently been reclad, while on the other side of the road we see the site of the then recently demolished Oxford Street School, which was soon replaced by the school hidden by the trees – Pilgrim Primary. On the skyline the tower and spire of St Peter's Church and the Roman Catholic Cathedral provide visual anchors for both images. *EH 02 June 2005*

GEORGE STREET "Plymouth Post War George Street 46/47" that's the caption on our Then picture (kindly supplied to us by Marilyn Endacott) and as you can see while the post-blitz rubble has been removed, there are still ruins in evidence here and there. While these damaged buildings were never destined to be rebuilt, like the shell of George Street Baptist Church on the right, above the post-box; some, like the Prudential Building on the left, were still serviceable but due for clearance as the new City Centre took shape. Although the building we are stood alongside – the Bank pub, formerly, of course, a bank – survived, it's out of view to our right, the only apparent link between the two images being the position of the lamp-post on our left. *EH 21 Jan 2006*

ROYAL PARADE So which is the Then and which is the Now, not too difficult probably but you never know! It's just over thirty years since our first picture was taken and one can't help but wonder just how long it will be before there is further change here, for the record though the "Now" picture is the one taken through the wire fencing! *EH 31 Jul 2004*

HOLIDAY INN Opened in 1970, the year of the Mayflower 350 celebrations, the Holiday Inn looks much the same today, thirty five years on, indeed, take the cars away and you would be hard pressed to put that amount of time between the images, except, of course, that the hotel has since become the Moat House. However one of the more interesting features of the comparison here is the difference between the motor cars, most notably the two Fords to the left of the foreground. Parked in the exact same space, both represent ground-breaking designs from their respect eras, the Ford Anglia from the sixties and Ford Ka from late nineties. On an even more incidental note, see how the belisha beacons have grown slightly in the intervening years. *EH 19 Mar 2005*

DRAKE CINEMA While it seems a shame to have lost a perfectly serviceable post-war Plymouth building, particularly one that held special memories for so many thousands, if not hundreds of thousands of patrons, the loss of the Drake Cinema has, visually at least been one of the most subtle changes on the 21st century Plymouth landscape. With the old Golden Hinde safely reinstated and the basic shape retained one could be forgiven for thinking that this was an elaborate make-over, rather than a wholesale demolition-and-rebuilding job. However in the nine years that separate these two images that is precisely what has happened. Less subtle of course, has been the replacement of the single storey car park and garage with the multi storey travel lodge and bars. *EH 05 Mar 2005*

KING STREET METHODIST CHURCH The original King Street Chapel, a Wesleyan foundation, stood on the corner of King Street and Tracy Street. The chapel itself and the upper floor of the adjacent Sunday School were destroyed by enemy bombing on the night of Friday 21 March 1941. In the subsequent Plan for the rebuilding of Plymouth no provision was made for the rebuilding of the church on the same site, indeed there was a suggestion that the War Damage compensation for King Street should be allocated to new premises at Crownhill. The decision was not popular with the Plymouth congregation and after much fuss it was decided to build a new church on another bomb site – a site previously occupied by numbers 11,12 and 13 the Crescent. Clearing of the new site began in early 1956 and the new premises were opened on 4th December 1957. The distinctive, brick-faced building stood for the best part of fifty years before changing social circumstances occasioned the demolition of the church and the erection of a number of 'Exclusive Retirement Apartments' – named Wesley Court to echo the site's previous use. *EH 24 Jun 2006*

LOCKYER STREET No.15 Lockyer Street became the Devon and Cornwall Homoeopathic Hospital and Three Towns Dispensary in 1893, less than thirty years after it had been built as a private residence. Absorbing two of its neighbours in 1911, the premises continued to serve the community as part of the health care provision for the area, for the next eighty years, apart from a brief period of closure (1941-2) after sustaining major damage in the Blitz. Finally closing in 1977 it was converted, in the early 1980s, into nineteen flats for the elderly by the Devon and Cornwall Housing Association. Both pictures courtesy of Doreen Mole from A Brief History of Plymouth Hospitals. *EH 22 Jan 2005*

HOE ROAD Our Then picture was supplied by P Le Bailly whose grandparents used to have a shop in neighbouring Notte Street. The old photograph was taken in pre-war Hoe Road and our visual fixing points are the three church towers - clearer perhaps in our Now view; St Andrew's, immediately to the left of the horse and carriage, St Matthias, a fairly indistinct blob on the old picture, just above and to the right of the boy, and Charles Church, which also punctuates the skyline, a short distance to the right of St Matthias as we see it here. While these three points help pull the images together, the modern street markings, the motor cars and the distinct lack of horse drawn vehicles tells us that a good many decades separate the two views. *EH 12 Mar 2005*

PIN LANE 'The most interesting domestic buildings still left in Plymouth are in Pin Lane' wrote RN Worth in his History of Plymouth, published in 1890. And when we see them here in our Then picture, kindly supplied by Bob Cook, it's easy to see why. At that time these were the only surviving examples in the town of the 'ancient arrangement of cellar and solar' – the cellar being accessed through the door at street level with the solar being a reference to the upper room. Clearly the changes here have been dramatic. The buildings on the left in the Then view - which were themselves late-nineteenth century redevelopments (Lucknow Place and Havelock Place) - are long gone, as are those interesting domestic buildings on the right. Indeed only the street plan, the building in the background on the other side of Southside Street and the Tudor building on the north-western corner (barely visible on our left) of Pin Lane remain little changed. *EH 17 Jun 2006*

ROYAL PARADE This was the devastated heart of Plymouth after the German bombers had left. The Guildhall Tower, in the centre, miraculously survived and the building on the right is a bank, now The Bank pub behind the Theatre Royal. The spire of St Andrew's Church can be seen, and in front of it is the shell of George Street Baptist Church, later pulled down. Out of this carnage was to come Royal Parade and newly-built stores as a new city centre rose out of the rubble. Today the same picture still shows the Guildhall Tower, now dwarfed by the Civic Centre building, and Royal Parade runs where the Baptist church once stood. On the right a corner of the Theatre Royal, opened in the early 1980's hides the surviving Bank building. *EH 26 Oct 1998*

ROYAL PARADE See the trees, how big they've grown … Over half a century separates these two images as we look back to the early fifties and an image taken just a dozen years after the 1941 Blitz. Many will remember the old National Provincial Bank and the post-war Costers, temporarily housed in a disguised (from the front elevation at least) Nissen hut. With Derry's Cross roundabout already laid out, but with no buildings yet constructed around it (apart from the Co-operative building out sight to our right), we have a clear view across Western Approach to the back of the Odeon. Obscuring the front of that building however is the newly completed GEC premises with the new Post Office just beyond it. *EH 07 May 2005*

MILLBAY PARK Well over thirty years separates the two images and yet at first glance you might be hard pressed to see any great difference. Look again though and apart from the changes to the rear of the Duke of Cornwall, take a good look at the area just to the left of that grand Victorian hotel - there, just visible above the hedge behind the football pitch, we see the roof of Millbay Station. Closed to all traffic by the early 1970s (passenger services had stopped in 1941) the railway buildings were demolished not that long after our Then picture was taken. For the keen eyed, there are other changes to be seen, but the other dominant feature, the tower of St Peter's appears little changed from this distance. *EH 24 Feb 2001*

CITADEL ROAD Like so many street scenes like this, separated by more than 30 years, the main changes are in what is happening on the road itself. There has been redevelopment of the bomb site, to the right of our Then picture and the odd structural alteration, like that to the end terrace of Citadel Road. But our early picture demonstrates a lack of cars, compared with today, and back Then there was not the same need for all the road markings and warnings. Few pupils to the new St Andrew's Primary School would have been driven to school when it first opened in 1961. Now although we can't see the school, we can see the safety measures - reflecting that there is more driving and less walking today. *EH 30 June 2001*

CITADEL ROAD A few alterations to the rear of John Betjeman's favourite Plymouth building – the Duke of Cornwall Hotel, a more modern version of the "Children Crossing" road sign, a few extra cars for the children to negotiate and improved street lighting, and there you have the principal differences to spot in this Then & Now pairing which sees us straddling a period of around thirty years – our Then picture dating from around 1969. Less obvious is the removal of some external pipes on the front elevation of these Citadel Road properties and the disappearance of the TV aerials, both of which help to give these splendid nineteenth century houses a little more of their original dignity. *EH 20 Aug 2002*

UNION STREET

It's difficult to line these two up precisely as, apart from elements of the road layout, there are no clear common reference points. However the footbridge across Union Street today does by and large, fall within the parameters of the older, much wider railway bridge that, until thirty-something years ago, straddled this part of the strip. Many will doubtless recall the old Central Restaurant, as it was styled in early 1960 when this view was taken. It stood just east of the bridge and had, certainly at that time, vending machines outside the premises, selling cigarettes – hence 'Players Please' – and chewing gum – Wrigley's of course. Note also the ad for Cadbury's 'all new chewy assortment - Lucky Numbers – 1/- (5p) a quarter' and the Bush Signs Austin van, the driver apparently engaged upon putting up some advertising material. *EH 19 Aug 2006*

WESTERN APPROACH With the prospect of more change, sooner rather than later, just south of the junction of Union Street and Western Approach, this truly marvellous pair of pictures beautifully illustrates the changes that have taken place here over the last thirty years. Although it's undated, our Then picture must have been taken just before the railway bridge over Union Street came down in 1974, along with the all the little businesses tucked under the arches - most of them motor-trade related - and the Central Taxis hut … and the Sweet Lemon Café on the other side of the road. Today, although there are few elements common to both to give us our bearings those elements are certainly conspicuous enough – most notably the old Odeon/Gaumont Cinema (Millennium Complex), and the Catholic Cathedral spire, sticking up just to the right of the Toys'r'Us logo. Note how remarkably close to the original railway bridge the new pedestrian crossing is from the car park to the Pavilions. *EH 02 Apr 2005*

GAUMONT It's a building that's been called a lot of things over the years; indeed three of those names can be seen here. Opened as the Gaumont Cinema in November 1931, it survived the war in one piece and was still operating as the Gaumont in 1949 when our Then photograph was taken – note the films being advertised; Dick Barton Special Agent and the Bandit of Sherwood Forest. In 1962 however the cinema was made smaller and in the process the stalls became the Majestic (Top Rank) Ballroom and the cinema was rebranded the Odeon. Implosion, Oceans, Waves and Monroes were other names used for successive reinventions of the dancehall, while after the cinema finally closed the whole building was refashioned, firstly as the Warehouse and latterly as the Millennium Complex … and the Boulevard. A victim of changing fashions it is currently closed and indeed has been for a year or two. *EH 26 Aug 2006*

PALACE THEATRE The tram lines have gone, new road markings have appeared and it would seem that the chap with the stop sign has been replaced by traffic lights, only it isn't a stop sign, it's an advertisement telling people they could get tuppence off Maypole Tea! Apart from the fashions and the nature of the transport though, remarkably little (from the outside at least) has changed in this stretch of Union Street – unlike the rest of this famous thoroughfare. It's all the more remarkable given that when the Then picture was taken the New Palace Theatre was still relatively new – as was the Great Western Hotel, with its massive street mounted advertising hoarding. However while the entertainment today in the Dance Academy is vastly different from that of the Palace in the 'Good Old Days', it's something at least that the fine old building is still standing! *EH 01 Apr 2006*

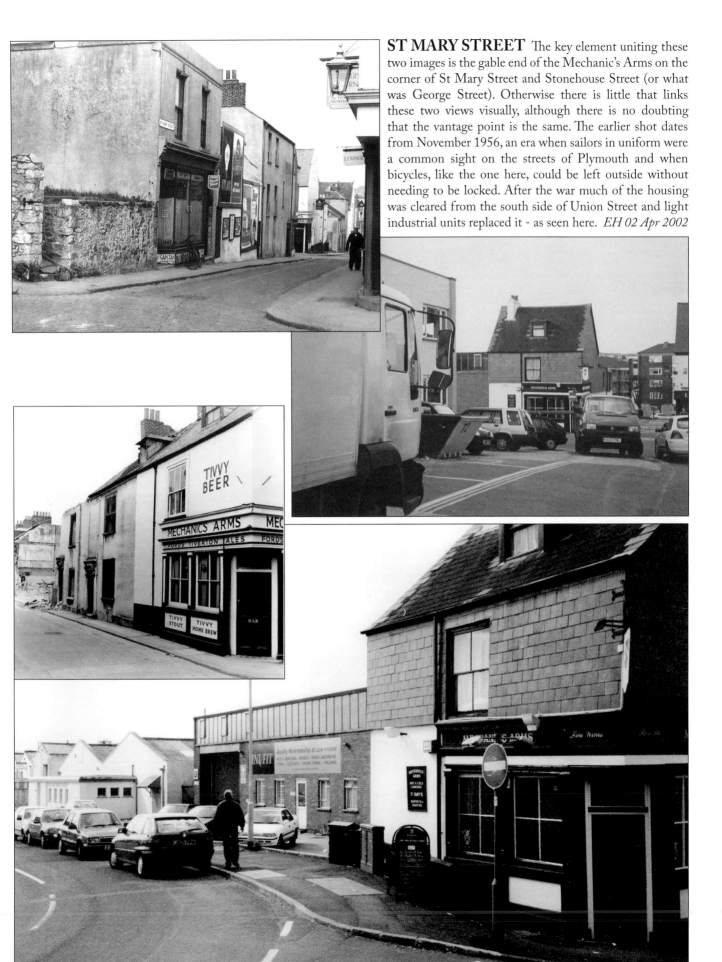

ST MARY STREET The key element uniting these two images is the gable end of the Mechanic's Arms on the corner of St Mary Street and Stonehouse Street (or what was George Street). Otherwise there is little that links these two views visually, although there is no doubting that the vantage point is the same. The earlier shot dates from November 1956, an era when sailors in uniform were a common sight on the streets of Plymouth and when bicycles, like the one here, could be left outside without needing to be locked. After the war much of the housing was cleared from the south side of Union Street and light industrial units replaced it - as seen here. *EH 02 Apr 2002*

MECHANIC'S ARMS Curiously enough with the slate hanging off the walls at first floor level our Now picture looks in some ways as if it could be older than our Then offering. But the older picture of these erstwhile George Street premises (they are now part of Stonehouse Street), actually dates from 1956. Back then, despite losing many neighbours in the Blitz this area was still dominated by residential properties. Now there are very few around here on the south side of Union Street, as commercial and industrial developments have been actively encouraged and favoured by the planners. *EH 02 Apr 2002*

ROYAL NAVAL HOSPITAL It was in 1910, some years after this old photograph was taken, that the gates of the former Royal Naval Hospital at Stonehouse were moved following an extension to the hospital grounds. The gates, still manned, now stand some 30 metres to the south of their original location, while the buildings on either side remain in their original position. Observe the trees, though, and see how much higher they have grown in the years that separate the two images. *EH 05 May 1998*

UNION STREET While the changes that have taken place in this particular part of Union Street over the last few decades appear little more than cosmetic, closer inspection reveals that Manor Street has been blocked off, so too, out of picture to the right, has Phoenix Street, directly opposite. Otherwise the main changes here in this, one of the few stretches of pre-war Union Street to survive pretty much intact, are in what is going on behind the facades. Ros Clothing has been gone for some time now, however the building is still occupied by Tom Roskell, where from time to time he exhibits his many and varied paintings of the area, some of them on a truly grand scale. Next-door Wilfred Searle, the Chemist, has moved on. Further along, just beyond the Octagon, the changes are more obvious. It will be interesting to see what the same view is like in another thirty years time. *EH 10 Mar 2001*

THE GRAND THEATRE Opened on Boxing Day 1889 with a production of Cinderella, the Grand Theatre in Union Street had converted to a cinema by the time it was hit by enemy bombs in the Second World War. Although the main body of the building was substantially intact the Grand never re-opened and, despite plans for its rebuilding in the fifties, it was finally pulled down in 1963. Alongside it the erstwhile Foresters Arms, which had become the Grand Theatre Hotel when the venue opened, still stands, although it too has now been closed for many years. From this angle the street looks remarkably consistent with its earlier appearance, west of this point however, only the former Royal Sovereign public house survives. *EH 29 Apr 2006*

MARTIN STREET In the days when the Three Towns were blessed with a number of large breweries this was the home of the Octagon Brewery. The view shows us the Martin Street aspect of the premises and, somewhat unusually all these years on, it is still possible to read the words "Octagon" and "Garage" on either side of John Benson's Car Electrical sign (which conveniently obscures the word "Brewery"). Compare with the sign where the lorry is parked in the old picture. Martin Street was the address of the brewery, known throughout the area for its familiar OB logo, a motif that can still be seen in one or two local pub windows, notably the Dolphin on the Barbican. *EH 05 May 1998*

EDGCUMBE STREET

Frederick Strang, boot repairer, had the shop to the left of the bomb-damaged group in the foreground, J Bremner had the general stores next door. This was, and still is, the end of Edgcumbe Street, Stonehouse. The vantage points for both shots are much the same, looking north west across the end of Stonehouse Bridge, towards the bottom end of the Brickfields. *EH 05 May 1998*

EDGCUMBE STREET The celebrated Paton Watson/ Abercrombie 1943 'Plan for Plymouth' spoke of the desire to demolish Union Street and have no building left standing that actually faced onto the revamped thoroughfare, a thoroughfare that would have housing on its northern side and industry to the south. As it transpired that wish was largely fulfilled, certainly up as far as the Palace Theatre and the Manor Street, Union Street's natural boundary between Plymouth and Stonehouse. There are, of course, a few original premises left on the northern side near that boundary, but the rest are long gone, as this comparison shows. Two hundred years ago, however, before Union Street's planner, John Foulston, had even visited the Three Towns, there was no route through this part of Stonehouse, the Plymouth road following the line of High Street/King Street. Edgcumbe Street, the bulk of what we see in the foreground here, was created to help give the growing town of Stonehouse the shopping centre it so badly needed, at the dawn of the nineteenth century. *EH 27 Aug 2005*

EAST STREET, STONEHOUSE The kerbstones are still in place, the cobbled road surface is little changed, for the most part, and off in the distance there is an unrendered wall that is substantially as it was fifty years ago and perhaps even a hundred years ago. Otherwise however there is little that is recognisable from our Then image of this stretch of East Street, Stonehouse. The pub signs, old and new, of the Lord High Admiral give us our location in both pictures, but the shop and the housing is long gone – a victim of the 1943 Plan for Plymouth that decreed that Stonehouse, south of Union Street, should be predominantly industrial and commercial, with domestic development concentrated on the northern side of the street. *EH 14 May 2002*

MILLBAY LAUNDRY Fronting onto Millbay Road and located between Hobart Street and Battery Street, Stonehouse was the "Millbay Laundry, Cleaning, Dyeing & Carpet Beating Works". Until comparatively recently the so-called Eddystone Works, the tall building to the left of the old view was still standing. Acquired in 1932 this was just one of several extensions the works underwent in the 1930s in what was perhaps the golden age for commercial laundry roundsmen. The wartime, too, added to the activity as many were they who in times of clothes rationing, would dye existing garments, either to give them a fresh lease of life, or to render them suitable as mourning wear. The early elevation we see here, incidentally, is of the works as they appeared not long after their completion in 1896. *EH 05 May 1998*

THE EARL GREY The old Earl Grey, bombed during the war, stood on the corner of Edgcumbe Street and Chapel Street, even though it was long regarded as part of the Union Street 'run ashore'. We see it here before the demolition men moved in to complete the job. In later years, a new pub rose on the site and for some time retained the old name. It was subsequently re-christened the Ha'penny Gate, an allusion to the nearby Stonehouse Bridge which for 155 years, until 1924, extracted that toll from pedestrians crossing it. Latterly known as the Brewery Tap, it is currently closed and boarded-up. It stood adjacent to the erstwhile Regent Brewery, and that building's end wall is clearly visible in both shots. *EH 05 Aug 2000*

DURNFORD STREET Looking across the top end of Durnford Street into Stonehouse Street presents us with a view which in places is older than the street names here. Prior to the war, standing in the same place we would have been looking across, what was then known as Chapel Street, into the entrance of George Street. Our Then picture, though, is very much post-war. It dates from 1975 and the redevelopment since then, on the other side of the trees, is not as obvious as the demolition which has seen the removal of the two nearest properties here and the impressive limestone building to the right. The flats on the edge of the roundabout have also had a facelift. *EH 26 Feb 02*

DURNFORD STREET The topography is the same: the buildings are completely different. Here we are just off the roundabout at the junction of Durnford Street, Edgcumbe Street, High Street and Stonehouse Bridge, looking down Durnford Street across the top of Newport Street. Once a thriving little thoroughfare with a few pubs, this is now the main entrance to the rapidly growing Marine Projects, one of the area's recent success stories. When our Then picture was taken in 1956, this stretch was part of Chapel Street. The boarded-up properties were not long for this world, however, and the changes reflect the general pattern prescribed by the 1943 Plan for Plymouth; that Stonehouse immediately south of Union Street would be developed for industry rather than housing. *EH 25 Aug 2001*

64

ROYAL MARINE BARRACKS

More than 100 years separate our two images of the late-eighteenth century Marine Barracks, and yet there is little indication of it. The fabric of the building is unchanged: only the road surface looks any different. It is not just the surface that has changed: it is the addition of the white lines and the double yellow lines that tell you time has moved on. You are also unlikely to see carts being pulled over cobbles around here these days (the cart is just outside the gate to the right). The octagonal post box outside the gate is long gone, although there is still a similar mid-Victorian box in the old Royal Naval Hospital. The uniform on the Marine at the gate is another clue: shirtsleeves rolled up to the elbow would not have been seen outside in those distant days! *EH 04 Mar 2000*

GEORGE STREET In the city centre, such incongruous comparisons are commonplace. At first glance, two pictures of George Street taken from the same vantage-point have little or no common ground – and that it is probably the ground alone that links these views. April 1957 is the date of our Then picture, and clearly the buildings we see in it are gone. Indeed the most obvious pre-1957 features in our Now picture, the spire of St. Peter's was not visible from here back then. So it is just the road itself, and even that has been resurfaced. Covered are the cobbles in Durnford Street and greatly widened is the erstwhile George Street (now Stonehouse Street). *EH 15 Oct 2002*

MILLBAY DOCKS It's difficult to date our badly damaged Then picture, but the similarities offered by these two aerial images of Millbay are too tempting to pass over. Note in the top right corner, long before the Ocean Court flats were built (in the early 1970s) the old Ocean Quay railway terminal is still in evidence. Similarly the foreground shows us what was still a fully working dock with no obvious concession to the leisure/pleasure side of seafaring. The grain silo itself, that seemingly immovable blot on the landscape was Then still in commission and Brittany Ferries were still a distant prospect. Perhaps closer examination will offer others more clues to the original date, the Now however is one of Herald picture editor, Pete Holdgate's wonderful shots from the recent Eye in the Sky supplement. *EH 07 Jan 2006*

MILLBAY DOCKS There's no date on our Then image but more than half a century has passed since it was taken and only those with long memories will recall the golden days of Plymouth as an Ocean-going port of call for liners and Plymouth's three much-loved tenders - seen here left to right – Sir Richard Grenville and Sir John Hawkins moored either side of the long-gone Princess Royal Pier pontoon and the Sir Francis Drake tied up alongside the now clear Millbay Pier. The latter was offered for sale back in April 1954 and was subsequently broken up on Marrowbone Slip alongside the China House at Sutton Harbour. There are plenty of other changes here too as Millbay, rather like Sutton Harbour itself, is gradually being converted away from a working waterfront towards an upmarket residential quarter of the city. *EH 27 May 2006*

DURNFORD STREET Some of the cosmetic work on the surface of Durnford Street is comparatively recent, and is part of the improvements of the Royal William Victualling Yard. Otherwise, the Now view is substantially the same as it has been since the church was completed – along with this end of Durnford Street and the Victualling Yard itself – shortly before Queen Victoria came to the throne. Interestingly, the window in the former Durnford Hotel was blocked out a hundred years ago – and possibly was even constructed like that. Essentially though, if you took away the cars and the signs designed for the motorists, there would be little difference between the two images. *EH 22 Jan 2000*

PRINCE GEORGE HOTEL With a sign pointing to the ARP Shelter down the steps at the side of Stonehouse Bridge and the white lines on the kerbstones to help in the blackout, you could be forgiven for thinking that this once-thriving Stonehouse hostelry was closed due to enemy action, but it wasn't. The other signs on the walls and in the windows tell a different story, for the Prince George was closed in 1939 with plans drawn up by Taylor & Bracken Architects of Tavistock Road and to be executed by Pearn Brothers Builders to transform the pub into an extension of the Plymouth Brewery building adjoining it. Today an extension of the Princess Yachts International complex occupies the same site. *EH 06 May 2006*

PLYMOUTH BREWERIES Gone – the distinctive brewery premises that also house the Prince George Hotel. Gone – the bottom of Edgcumbe Street, the western end of Union Street and gone too, much of the old street furniture on Stonehouse Bridge. But the bridge is still there, of course, as are the steps down to the water on the seaward side – the other side having been infilled more than thirty years ago. The comparison also allows us to see how Princess Yachts have left a walkway on the edge of the harbour wall here and to see that the sea wall itself is much the same. Note the changes on the drinking front though; beer for 6d (2.5p) and Pale Ale with 'no sediment' – signs of the time, quite literally. *EH 15 April 2006*

STONEHOUSE BRIDGE Stonehouse Bridge – 1937 and today. The road surface has changed, the tramlines are gone, the pedestrians are fewer and the cars are more plentiful, as certain aspects of life continue to change. Gone are the advertising hoardings promoting new films and products, because fewer people go to the cinemas and so the advertisers, like Guinness on the far right, concentrate on the small screen, which has largely superseded the cinema. The Army Recruiting Office, here on the left at the end of Richmond Walk, is also long gone: meanwhile, the planting of trees has significantly softened the old defensive lines of Devonport. *EH 26 Mar 2002*

STONEHOUSE BRIDGE We have featured this view before, when our Then picture took us back about 100 years. In that image, there was the old brewery building to the right of the view on the edge of Stonehouse Pool. Here our Then picture only takes us back about 15 years, but look at the differences. Since then, Marine Projects has developed on the brewery site to become one of the bigger employers in Plymouth. Beyond it, although we can't see it from this vantage point, all those old Edgcumbe Street properties, at this end of Union Street, have been demolished and this stretch is now much wider and more open. But the boat huts in the foreground look much the same as before, and from them alone you would be hard pressed to tell which was Then and which is Now. *EH 20 Jan 2001*

DEVONPORT HILL

See the trees how big they've grown, not that surprising really when sixty years separates the two images. Our Then picture dates from April 1937; when cobbled streets were commonplace; when trams were still running in Plymouth, when there was an Army Recruiting Office at the entrance to Richmond Walk; when there was a clear view of the Military Families Hospital (behind the bus) on the north side of Devonport Hill and when the Hippodrome, the Savoy and the Palace Theatre were among the top entertainment venues in the city. No television or video machines to compete with then, hence the appearance at the Palace, for the first time in Plymouth, of "The World Looks Up" four shows in one – Revue, Radio, Variety and Cabaret. Another big difference, although not a visible one, is that in 1937 water still flowed under this bridge. Now it's all changed and even double-decker buses are a rare sight out here these days. *EH 17 Jul 1999*

KING'S ROAD

The view today is a familiar enough one. Look through the tree-lined King's Road from Stonehouse Bridge across to the old Devonport Technical College, with the multi-storey blocks of the College of Further Education now dominating the skyline to the right. But how has it changed? Turn the clocks back 60 years and there are many traces of a past life now gone – the cobbles in the road surface have given way to a smooth tarmac finish; the tram lines are long gone; the London and South Western Railway Line to the Ocean Quay terminal, seen here snaking along King's Road, has long since closed down (to passengers in 1910 and goods traffic in 1966); and the water on the northern side of the bridge was in-filled in the early 70's. It is interesting to note how many of the products are being advertised are still available; among them Oxo, Vim, Bovril, Ovaltine, Gilbey's spirits and White Line whiskey. Sadly, Underhills, in Frankfort Street, no longer exists, a legacy of wartime devastation that was to make little long-term visual impact on this particular part of town. *EH 04 Sept 1999*

RICHMOND WALK Thanks to Anne Tolley for this pairing. This corner of Richmond Walk has seen a good many changes over the years but in behind it all for many decades Blagdon's boatyard has been a hardy survivor. It was in 1809 that Richmond Walk was first created around the waterfront from Stonehouse Bridge to Mutton Cove and various buildings and enterprises have come and gone in the meantime (among them the Royal Clarence Baths, Victoria Cottages and Ocean Quay Railway Terminus 1877-1966). Note how part of the harbour wall remains, and how the tide is much further out in our Now picture, and although the houses, the baths and the original signal station at Mount Wise have gone, the new 'Mast' development has replaced it on the top of the mount. *EH 08 Apr 2006*

RICHMOND WALK It's hardly the most picturesque part of Plymouth, particularly from this angle, but it's fascinating none the less and the views in other directions near here are quite special. We're looking along Richmond Walk; in our Then picture we see the old railway line to Ocean Quay Station, a line that was used for goods traffic until 1966 – some nine years after this photograph was taken. Long since filled in, this side of the road is now quite flat. The road itself however follows the same line as it always has and a key building in equating the two scenes is the one with the distinctive roof and white chimney, to the left of the SGB sign in our Now shot – if you can find it in our Then picture the other elements will fall into place. *EH 03 Nov 2001*

KING'S ROAD It was on 7 September 1964 that King's Road railway station at Devonport was last used by a passenger train. Goods services however continued for a further seven years but then, after almost 95 working years, it was shut down completely. The year before the station's closure the College of Further Education was established in the city, and it wasn't long before building work began here on developing a campus for the college, which, thirty years on is still expanding. Note the prime element linking the two images is the erstwhile Devonport Tech – opened in 1897 as the Devonport Municipal Science, Art and Technical Schools building. *LK 19 Nov 2005*

VICTORIA PARK The caption on the back of our "Then" picture (kindly supplied by Peter Waterhouse) reads "Victoria Park, Plymouth 1947 – note the old viaduct bridge and bandstand. The bridge has now been demolished." Certainly at first glance it is hard to make out these features and as far as the park itself appears there is very little change from that day to this. And as the Park celebrates its centenary this year it is fair to say that there has been comparatively little change here in the last 100 years. However prior to that time we would have been standing on the side of the Millbridge looking at the highest reaches of Stonehouse Creek, up towards the site of the old bridge at Pennycomequick. Look carefully though and there are many little changes here, most notably the tower block alongside North Road Station, the newish developments in front of it and the Richard Deacon sculpture that sits atop the columns of the former railway bridge. *EH 15 Jan 2002*

WILTON STREET No need for double-yellow lines then for although it always has been a major thoroughfare Wilton Street wasn't anywhere near as busy then as it is these days. More than fifty years separates these two images and yet take away the cars and strip back the tarmac and it all looks pretty similar today – apart from the odd television aerial and the rather taller lampposts. Incidentally, although it's not that easy to spot, it's hard to imagine anyone leaving a bicycle propped up against the kerb these days, certainly without it being chained to a tree or a post - here or anywhere else for that matter. *EH 25 June 2002*

MOUNT WISE Those who know the place probably know it well, it will be a part of Plymouth they enjoy revisiting from time to time. For many others this may well be an as yet undiscovered delight – Mount Wise. Behind our vantage point is the impressive memorial to Robert Falcon Scott, in front of us the Hamoaze and the comparatively new Mount Wise Mast – a fabulous lookout point offering stunning views of Plymouth and Cornwall. Architecturally designed to mirror the old signalling mast here, as seen in our Then picture, it is hard now to picture the naval housing block, Onslow House, that stood here for a number of decades in the intervening years that separate these two images. *EH 30 Apr 2002*

DEVONPORT TECHNICAL SCHOOL Arriving at exactly the same spot that the earlier photographer had occupied just over 100 years before there was little to indicate the passage of time. Hence the wait until the arrival on the scene of some marker to show that one of these pictures was taken in 1999, and just in case you're playing spot the difference it's the car not the bird flying past the clock tower that I was waiting for. Otherwise it is quite remarkable how little altered this view is. Always an educational establishment the nature of the teaching inside the building has changed greatly over the years but the exterior fabric remains much as it was when it was opened as Devonport's Municipal Science, Art and Technical Schools in 1899. Like its long-gone counterpart in Plymouth, this was Devonport's way of marking one of Queen Victoria's jubilees. The building here commemorated the monarch's "60 years glorious reign" (the foundation stone was laid in 1897), while the Plymouth building had, ten years earlier, marked the Golden Anniversary. Incidentally, among the original occupants of this building (from 1898 to 1936) were the girls of Devonport's Municipal Secondary School, which upon its removal to its present premises (in 1937) became Devonport High School for Girls. Currently the building serves as an annexe of the neighbouring College of Further Education. *EH 10 Jul 1999*

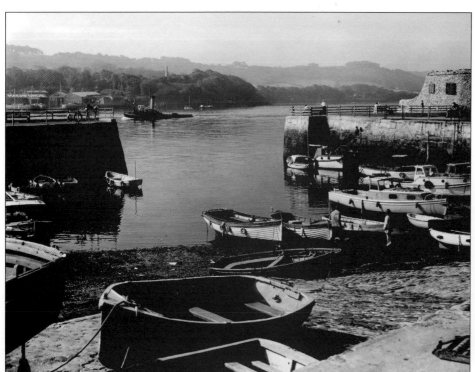

MUTTON COVE Time was when Mutton Cove was one of the principal routes into Cornwall. There were inns, shops, houses and ferryboats – and plenty of them. But that era has long since passed, and to an extent for the last 40 years, or so, time almost appears to have stood still here. Even the boats don't look that different, and the distant view is much the same, although the name Mashfords is no longer emblazoned in big letters on the roof of the boatyard buildings at Cremyll. *EH 24 Mar 2003*

DEVONPORT COLUMN

With so much of old Devonport bombed or redeveloped over the last sixty years or so it's always refreshing to find a corner that is little changed. Those who know Ker Street will know that the Town Hall, the Oddfellows Hall and the Column form a group that has dominated that street for almost two hundred years. Tucked in behind that group however there is this, albeit less-obvious and certainly less imposing view of the column that, despite all the attendant redevelopment around Ker Street, Duke Street and Monument Street, still carries visual and structural echoes of the past. *EH 08 Jan 2002*

DEVONPORT MEMORIAL The survival of this unusual memorial at the entrance to Devonport Park suggests that there has been little change here opposite the charming little Swiss lodge. But look again and you will see how the planting around the memorial has gone and most of the greenery within. Also the trumpeting figurines have disappeared as has the muscular figure supporting the fountain-head. Still clearly visible though are the names of the ships' companies who contributed towards this memorial for a man who did sterling work to improve the social position of seamen and marines – Admiral Sir Charles Napier. Napier died in 1860, just two years after Devonport Park, one of the first and finest public parks in the country, had been opened. Within three years the memorial had been completed. The early photograph is pre-war and in it we can see the south-west corner of Granby barracks – now long gone. *EH 20 Mar 1999*

DEVONPORT PAVILION The Park Pavilion in Devonport Park still looks splendid today, it now serves as a residential home. In former times this grand building contained the residence of the Park Keeper. At one time this was a Mr Baker, who, according to Gerald Barker, in his "Days in Devonport Part VI" ... "was very strict and well-respected by the boys and girls who played in the park". The figures around the former fountain however are not in such good shape. The central feature has gone entirely, of the four standing ladies only two headless figures remain, and they look like replacements, as indeed do the ornate flower pots around the edge. Behind the pavilion in the older picture incidentally, which dates from the 1890s, we can see a part of the original Granby Barracks, long since demolished to make way for housing.

DEVONPORT PARK The similarities between today's two pictures belie the changes seen from this vantage point over the past 60 years. The wall that marks the boundary of the old Gun Wharf (Morice Yard) still stands prominent at the western end of Devonport Park, but the main road from Devonport to Keyham, which ran along side it, has been replaced by Park Avenue, which cut a swathe through the park in the post-war redevelopment of the area. An extension to Keyham Yard swallowed up parts of Moon Street, William Street, Mooncove Street, and Charlotte Street, aspects of which we can see here to the right of the picture. Today, where once substantial blocks of housing stood, we see the more modern parts of Keyham Yard – below the Frigate Complex and to the right of the bridge that now connects Morice Yard and Keyham. *EH 06 Feb 1999*

THE ARK ROYAL Not a great deal of Fore Street survived the war … on either side of the wall that was to divide the thoroughfare in the fifties. The Ark Royal itself was a new build on the site of the former Devonport Railway Hotel and was first opened in 1957 – two years after the last HMS Ark Royal was launched. Forty years later, after a period of closure, the pub re-opened as the Zoo Rooms. In the meantime the empty space to the left had been infilled, parts of the west side of Chapel Street had been demolished and the recently re-clad tower blocks had been built in the heart of Devonport. One can but wonder what the next forty years holds for the area. *EH 06 Oct 2001*

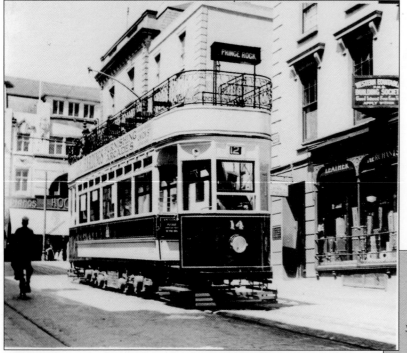

CHAPEL STREET Chapel Street, Devonport, looking towards Fore Street. The angles aren't quite right - the street curves around to the left rather more than it used to – but we aren't too far from the spot where our pre-war, tram-era photographer would have been standing. Then, the old Devonport Post Office would have been to his right, Now, a long grey wall, encompassing the 1950s southern dockyard extension runs along most of the western side of Chapel Street. But not for much longer. Then, Devonport was a vibrant town in its own right, Now, for too long deprived of that vitality, it is looking forward to a new lease of life, as redevelopment brings with it an opportunity to recapture some of its erstwhile glory. *EH 05 Feb 2005*

FORE STREET At first glance perhaps there seems little to connect the two images – but look again and take your bearings first from the Forum. Opened in 1938 the Forum is one of the few pre-war survivors in Fore Street, Devonport – most of this area was destroyed in the Blitz. There are a couple of early Fore Street buildings that remain along from the Western Hotel on the other side there is only the Forum – on this side of the dockyard wall. Look carefully at the Now picture, however, and along from the Forum and in line with it, you can see the group of buildings that appear above the car that is heading towards us in the Then shot. Who knows, perhaps one day, in the not-too-distant future, as the fate of the dockyard unfolds, the two halves of this street may yet be reunited. Fore Street was once Devonport's principle thoroughfare and the building on the far left in the older picture is the grand Devonport Post Office, designed by George Wightwick and opened in 1849. *EH 25 Sep 2004*

MORICE SQUARE At first glance the similarity may not be obvious but if you focus your attention on the area just above the lone car in the old picture you will see the distinctive windows of the Royal Fleet Club off Morice Square and you'll see the same tree, much bigger now, but still obscuring a part of that view. Of course in the old photo we don't get to see much of the tree because of that part of Morice Street, between Cannon Street and the Square, that was still standing, albeit only just, as clearly it had been recently damaged by enemy bombing. *EH 05 May 1998*

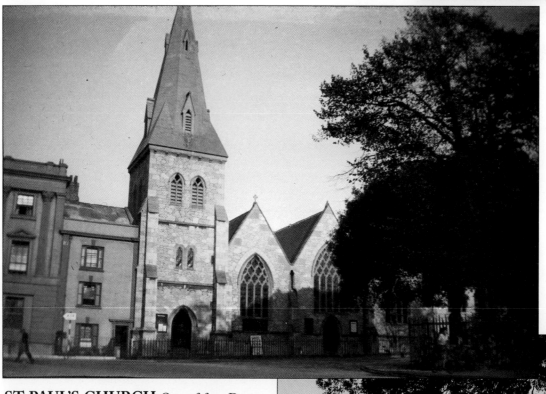

ST PAUL'S CHURCH One of four Devonport churches designed by J Piers St Aubyn in the early 1850s, St Paul's Church, Morice Street was; like its contemporaries St Stephen's and St James', destroyed during the Blitz; only St Mary's survived. After the war the church authorities decided that one church was enough and so it fell upon the older St Aubyn's church to serve the needs of the Anglicans in the old part of Devonport. In this rare prewar picture taken from the Warren archives, we see St Paul's across Morice Square: Then, as Now, one of the larger open areas of public space in the built-up part of the old town. *EH 21 May 2005*

TORPOINT FERRY It was walk-on-walk-off. Now it's drive-on-drive-off! Our 1890 travellers had to walk down a pebbled beach to travel across the Tamar on the Torpoint passenger ferry. Now smooth slipways on either side guide motorists on to the three ferries that cross the river daily. Our Now picture shows the new 'stretched' ferry, which can accommodate five lanes of vehicles.

CHARLOTTE STREET

Clearly the most obvious changes here in Charlotte Street itself are those on the east side of the road where the old terraced houses, still mirrored on this side of the street, have long since been replaced by modern accommodation. Long gone is Percy Lang, 'turf commission agent', and the boot repair business of Frederick C Moore, located just beyond the two cars. It's the other vehicles that make this March 1958 Then view particularly interesting though, as we see a lone Jeep at the bottom and a large number of military vehicles in the post-war, pre-wall area on the other side of Albert Road. *EH 22 Oct 2002*

CHARLOTTE STREET It's a familiar enough story in any part of Plymouth, indeed any part of Britain, over the last forty years or so as so many smaller shops have disappeared from our older streets as the superstores and supermarkets with their cheaper prices and massive car parks have made it impossible for the little independent retailer. Here in Charlotte Street however there are possibly other factors to consider as the shop in the foreground here was primarily a tobacconist and a gents hairdressers, situated not too far from a busy Dockyard entrance, Albert Road. The closure of that entrance and the decline in the number of dockyard workers and the decline in the number of smokers probably all played their part. Otherwise apart from the increase in car ownership there are few major differences in these two views separated by over forty years. *EH 21 May 2002*

CHARLOTTE STREET Plymouth doesn't seem to have quite as many advertising hoardings as some cities but here's one site that has seen many years service, on the corner of Charlotte Street and Albert Road. Of the 1950s advertisements the heavily promoted Ovaltine ("for Vitality") is probably better known than Ricory – "Cuts coffee time costs … 2/6d (12p) makes 48 cups". Above these poster ads there is the somewhat longer-lived lettering promoting Baskerville's Bakery and Hovis Bread. H Baskerville and Son were based at 45 Charlotte Street, and others may recall CH Baskerville's bakery in Godolphin Terrace. *EH 27 Aug 2002*

HADDINGTON ROAD Width of carriageway 22 feet 9 inches, width of the footpath – 9 feet; the job of the street lighting was therefore to light under rather than through the trees and as you can see the old gas lights in Haddington Road were not nearly as high as the modern electric lighting, but then, of course, neither were the trees quite as tall as they are now. There were, however undoubtedly more of them – and equally undoubtedly … a lot fewer motorcars. Indeed it's hard now to imagine this street being traffic free, even were it to be closed off for a street party! *EH 13 Aug 2002*

FULLERTON ROAD Like so many other Plymouth streets these days, it is almost impossible to imagine them as car-free as Fullerton Road appears in our Then picture. However, strip away the cars from the Now view and it becomes much more difficult to spot the changes that have taken place here over the last 50 years. But they are there – among them the road surface itself; the disappearance of those high pole-mounted washing lines and tree growth to our right; the replacement of the old window patterns as double-glazing spreads along the street; and the change from gas to electric lighting. What other changes can you see? *EH 19 Mar 2002*

ST. LEVAN'S GATE 1910 is the date on the back of the old photo and although St Levan's Gate has been greatly widened it is still possible to pick out many common features in the two pictures. The tram lines have gone, along with the overhead wires, so, too, have the distinctive chimney stacks along with the dockyard bell and the large workshop behind the re-roofed building on the other side of the wall. Look carefully at the old picture and, to the left of the tram, you might just make out a female street-seller with her basket of wares. *EH 05 May 1998*

KEYHAM ROAD Almost half a century separates these two images and, while they are unmistakably similar in many respects, the changes are obvious too. The Keppel's Head, with its formerly distinctive tiled frontage, has long been part of the larger Complex pub, while the neighbouring Prince of Wales closed more than ten years ago. In between the two, the former Greenburgh Brothers premises is now the Temptations lap-dancing club. Note also the changes in car design and the complete lack of cobbles now! *EH 30 May 2003*

AVONDALE ARMS At first glance the passing of almost 50 years separating these two images seems to have had little impact. There are a few extra traffic markings and lights - but let's look again. The Avondale holds the key standing clear and proud in both pictures. It has changed comparatively little from the outside - and why should it? Inside, any changes and refurbishments don't detract from the fact that Arthur Squire has put in more than 50 years here as licensee, from 1950 onwards, and he has seen this junction change in many subtle ways. St Levan's Gate, once a principal entrance to the dockyard, no longer witnesses major coming and goings, and yet the traffic here, running at right angles to St Levan's Road, is greater than ever. Note too the infill, to the right of the pub - those buildings have been here for a long time now, but they were not there in 1956 when our Then shot was taken. *EH 30 Jun 2001*

ALEXANDRA ROAD

Alexandra Road, Ford, near the Dockyards and the blitzed out St Levan's Road, had its share of bomb damage too. Here, the Ford Hotel, on the corner of the west end of Alexandra Road, was bombed out - but it was also the first licensed house to be rebuilt in Plymouth. When Ford was first laid out in the middle of the last century Keyham Lake would have come as far inland as the top of St Levan's Road and the "ford" would have been the most westerly pedestrian crossing point. *EH 15 Sep 1997*

KEYHAM VIADUCT One of many 'Before and After' image pairings to appear in 'Keyham – The Past Brought Back To Life' is this set featuring part of the old London and South Western Railway Viaduct. The second viaduct to be built over the St Levan valley, the L&SW was 'completed in 1890 by 2,000 navvies under Sir John Jackson'. Closed 74 years later it wasn't until January 1987 that work began on its demolition, opening up large tracts of land for development on both sides of the valley. *EH 04 Mar 2006*

RAGLAN GATE Raglan Barracks gatehouse, Then – when the barracks were still very much operational at the beginning of the twentieth century and Now – boarded up and awaiting a buyer. Thanks to George Williams for both images. The barracks were declared out of date by the War Office back in 1937 and plans for their demolition were set in motion. They survived another thirty years however, latterly seeing service as the Headquarters for some of Plymouth's Territorial and Auxiliary Force units. Today only the long-neglected gatehouse remains an imposing 1850s structure at the entrance to Plymouth Albion's car park at the Brickfields. Incidentally it's hard to imagine the health and safety people allowing men and women to stand on open roof tops these days! *EH 22 Jul 2006*

WARLEIGH AVENUE Warleigh Avenue and a street that no longer exists - Hamilton Street - in the Keyham area, suffered a major Blitz attack in the Second World War. On August 26 in 1940 some homes were were bombed to the ground while others were left in such a state that they later had to be pulled down. The area was vulnerable - close to the dockyard, a prime target for the German bombers, and just round the corner from the densley-populated St Levan's Road, which also suffered in the raids. Our wartime picture shows people making their way through the rubble, or picking over whatever remains of their possessions in their former homes. *EH 15 Sep 1997*

91

OLD VIADUCT It is hard to imagine that 150 years ago, this valley had green fields either side of a large tidal inlet that ran the length of what is now St Levan Road, and which was once known as Keyham Lake Road. The first houses here were built to accommodate the workforce of the newly-built Keyham Steamyard in 1850s. Before that decade was out, the first railway viaduct over the now in-filled lake was built. Rebuilt several times since, it still stands today, unlike the later St Levan Road or Ford Viaduct, which came down at the end of the 1980s and which had been officially opened in May 1890. New housing has since filled the scar created by the removal of the seven-arched construction, and now it is hard to remember just how and where it ran. *EH 06 Jan 2001*

HMS DRAKE Royal Naval Barracks, Devonport, better known these days as HMS Drake, seen here in the old picture dating from the mid-1980s just a few years after the barracks were opened but before they were completed. At this stage the impressive wardroom building, begun in Victoria's Diamond Jubilee year, 1897, had yet to be built as did the clock tower of 1896 which just stands proud above the skyline. It is perhaps harder now to discern those features as today there is little land left in this view that has not been developed, but vantage points are almost identical as can be seen from that short stretch of road visible just outside the front entrance of the barracks today. *EH 05 May 1998*

CAMEL'S HEAD CREEK Time was when there were two railway lines running across Camel's Head Creek and it was from the bridge of the one surviving (originally the Great Western Line) that the Now picture was taken. That bridge, the Weston Mill Viaduct, now looks out over dry land where once the waters of the old creek ebbed and flowed. On that land the Navy has extended its Naval Base, as the Submarine Refit Complex now has its main entrance (and a large car park), here, fed directly by an offshoot from the parkway. The two other bridges are long gone, as is the line that carried the London and South Western Railway. Most of the houses are still standing today, though, and a good many more besides, but note how some of those in the front line fell victim to road widening and local traffic flow improvements. *EH 05 May 1998*

ST BUDEAUX STATION It's hard now to believe that St Budeaux was once served by two railway stations, particularly as the site of one (the old London & South Western) is now in the middle of a busy junction where Wolseley Road meets Victoria Road and Trelawney Place. Long gone are all the buildings in our Then photo – a charming wartime period piece. I wonder how many of them went to see the Mickey Rooney/Judy Garland feature advertised here. Released in 1940, Strike Up The Band, also featuring the Paul Whiteman Orchestra, was showing at Devonport's Electric Cinema. *EH 05 May 1998*

SHELLEY WAY Take away the traffic, and the original lamp-stands, and there are few clues to tell you that half a century separates these two images. We're standing at the junction of Shelley Way with Collin Close, St Budeaux, and although there is a little variation in the vegetation there really is a little in the way of permanent features to distinguish our Then and Now pictures. One can only wonder at what this view might look like in another 50 years. *EH 22 Mar 2003*

PETERS PARK LANE The more interesting comparison would doubtless have been between our then picture and the same view ten years or so earlier when all this would have been green fields, but here we are at the dawn of the 1950s looking down Peters Park Lane, St Budeaux, lined with young trees and not a car in sight. Note too the old light fittings – then considered state-of-the-art and the Thelwell-style telegraph pole on which you can easily imagine a number of small birds perched. *EH 12 Jul 2003*

SALTASH PASSAGE The changes aren't immediately obvious, neither are they all that major, but some thirty-five years separates these two images and during that time the Tamar Road Bridge, which was new when our Then pic was taken, has been significantly extended, although from this angle it's rather hard to tell! A few houses have been added and here, outside the Ferry House Inn, we see chairs and picnic tables on the slip way of the old ferry route. *EH 06 Dec 2003*

SALTASH PASSAGE

Our Then picture dates back some eighty-five years and remarkably enough the youngest of the three people on the carriage is still with us. Florence Johns was born in 1917 and is seen here with her father Fred Johns and sister Winifred, outside what was then their family home in Saltash Passage. Fred was a well-known fruiterer in St Budeaux and had a small-holding off Wolseley Road overlooking the Kloof. As you can see the house here, currently in the hands of Guy Osborne has undergone quite a transformation, with several intermediate stages having taken place along the way. Incidentally note how all these years on the public street light is still in the same place only now it stands taller and casts its light further afield. *EH 31 Dec 2005*

TAMAR & BRUNEL BRIDGES

The postmark on the picture postcard is dated August 1966 and looking at the cars that would be about right, the image probably being a fairly new one for that summer. The Tamar Road Bridge had only been open for five years at that time and little could the road users then have imagined that forty years later the volume of traffic would justify creating new lanes either side of the main structure. Meanwhile Brunel's magnificent single-track railway bridge continues to take trains to and from Cornwall almost 150 years after it first opened in 1859. *EH 29 Apr 2005*

TAMAR BRIDGE Almost 40 years separate these two images, yet there are remarkably few changes. But that will not be the case for much longer. The toll-booths in Roy Todd's Then picture have been replaced, and the centre of the roundabout has been reduced in size. Both photographs show the bridge in different stages of development. Our Then shot shows it just prior to completion ahead of its official opening in 1961. The Now picture shows it in the recent second stage of development, with the addition of extra lanes on either side of the structure. *EH 21 Oct 2000*

SALTASH FERRY It was October 23, 1961, when Roy Todd slipped down to Saltash to take this rare picture. The sun was beginning to set and, later that evening, five sky rockets would be fired across the night sky, marking the last ever trip of the Saltash Ferry. At the bar of the Ferry House Inn, licensee Mike Goulding was quoted as saying that the inn would keep its present name. Almost 40 years on and the Ferry House Inn is still there, name unchanged. And as for the ferry itself, that's still in service too - not here, though. However, if you've ever travelled across the Fal on the King Harry Ferry you may well recognise this craft. Meanwhile, note how little the layout of Saltash Passage (far right) has changed since 1961. *EH 04 Sep 2000*

TAMAR WAY King's Tamerton is there to our left, the early fifties development of Harewood Crescent to our right, the brambles in the foreground quite possibly marking the beginning of what was known as Scratchy Face Lane. Beyond the brambles the wide open expanse, which from the 1943 Plan for Plymouth onwards was earmarked for the Parkway and which, in the event, was not laid out until the 1980s. Intriguingly, away in the distance you can just make out on the old picture, the temporary post-war development known as Tamar Way. Lined either side with pre-fabs, these were not replaced with more permanent housing when they were eventually demolished, unlike most housing of this kind. *EH 05 May 1998*

BLUE MONKEY Although it is no longer the main road through Plymouth to the Tamar Bridge, Crownhill Road is still busier than it was 40 years ago, when our Then picture was taken. The pub, though, is not busy. Closed for some time now and re-named the St Budeaux Inn a few years ago, the Blue Monkey was built as the Church Inn many moons ago. It first became the St Budeaux Inn back in the St Budeaux Inn back in the 19th century. St Budeaux Church, with its timeless tower, is where Sir Francis Drake married Mary Newman and it is close by the pub. *EH 29 Nov 2003*

CARESWELL AVENUE "Careswell Avenue, Ham No.1 Estate, Devonport" is the location as specified on our Then picture and as with so many other older pictures of residential parts of Plymouth there can be no escaping the fact that the biggest obvious difference between these two images, separated by over fifty years, is generated by the fact that, back in 1950 comparatively few households possessed a motor car, whereas today the vast majority of them have at least one. The Then picture here, incidentally was taken by a gas board official, the street lighting here was then gas – "Mounting height 15 feet, spacing 105 feet, type of lamp Sugg "8000", type G. 2 lt. No.2 mantles complete with controller, Comet Igniter and two way reflectors". *EH 12 Feb 2002*

DRYBURGH CRESCENT   At first glance it almost looks like the pictures could have been taken on the same day, before everyone had gone out for the day and after they had just left, but actually it's not fifty minutes that separates the two images but more like fifty years! Back then comparatively few people in Plymouth owned a car, now it seems most people do … or at least most families do. Fifty years ago Dryburgh Crescent itself was fairly new and as you can see from the width of the road, the planners, even then, didn't really anticipate that cars would one day be parked on both sides of the road. That apart though and one or two changes in the surrounding green belt there are few obvious differences. It's hard to imagine an unattended freestanding bicycle being parked on the kerb like that anywhere in town now though, not unless it was chained to a lamppost! *EH 11 Aug 2001*

MALMESBY CLOSE This quiet cul-de-sac on the Ham estate was fairly new when our "Then" picture was taken some fifty odd years ago, but apart from the cars, telegraph poles and the odd television aerial, there isn't that much change on the face of it. The greenery is different, some of the trees have matured, some have gone and the hedges in front of the houses have filled out, but that's about it. There is something more, electric lighting has long-since replaced the elegant Sugg 8000 type G 2 gas lamps. Do you remember them? Well now you know what they were called! *EH 16 Jul 2002*

HAM DRIVE The road layout here at Ham Drive was fairly new, but the planting quite mature when our Then picture was taken back in the early 1950s. Remarkably though, there is little to show the passing of the time, apart from the street furniture - the lamposts, the telegraph pole, the road markings, signs and the pavements. Closer inspection reveals a few changes in the foliage and it's fun to 'spot the difference' in the trees and bushes. *EH 30 Jun 2001*

MILEHOUSE Written on the back of our Then picture (kindly loaned by Pete Waterhouse) is the following: "Milehouse, Plymouth, which has just been resurfaced. Below the Embassy is Underwoods Stores; next door to them is Embassy Café. Note how clear the area is, and no traffic lights." The picture is dated – 1949. Move the clock on half a century and really the principal changes here are on that road surface, as lights, barriers and signage have all been introduced to direct and calm the much greater volume of traffic which now uses this busy junction. Remarkably, there is not a single car in the earlier picture: just one van and a flat-back lorry. Now when did you last see one of those delivering anything other than scaffolding?

ALMA ROAD A note on the back of Peter Waterhouse's Then picture reads, "Alma Road leading into Pennycomequick 1947 – note the lack of traffic and the wide pavements – so different from today." So different indeed, as here the road junction has been developed to such a great extent that where, fifty years ago, there were no road markings. Now this particular stretch is for westbound traffic only, the eastbound lanes running over what was then part of Central Park. Certainly now it is hard to imagine any time during the hours of daylight when you might see so little traffic on this stretch. *EH 23 July 2002*

CENTRAL PARK PADDLING POOL Doubtless our Then picture will evoke many happy memories for Plymouth parents and a number of young people approaching their fortieth birthdays. July 1973 is the date on this picture of the children's paddling pool in Central Park. For those having trouble placing it, that's St Bartholomew's in the background – note all the building work under way today, on the other side of Outland Road. On this side too there have been changes as the whole Milehouse corner of Central Park was eaten into some years ago to accommodate the new traffic arrangements. More obviously of course, the paddling pool has gone and in its place today, a designated skateboard area, quite a good one too. *EH 19 Jan 2005*

PLYMOUTH ZOO Opened in April 1962 Plymouth Zoo was home to hundreds of animals for more than sixteen years. Lions, giraffes, hippos, elephants and penguins were among the varied range of species kept here by the Chipperfield family. However as the seventies progressed numbers dwindled and the zoo closed to the public in 1978 - although it continued to be used as an animal quarantine area for a brief while after that. Within a few years however all signs had vanished and the site enjoyed a brief existence as a skateboard park. Now that too has gone and the area has been returned to parkland. *EH 1999*

PA BOX It's one of the few pre-main stand structures left at Home Park, although it's changed considerably since Jumbo Chisholm led the promotion side of 1952 out onto the pitch. Time was when the Directors occupied the open air upstairs area, now appropriately known as the Chisholm Lounge and the PA Box was alongside it to the left as we look at it – now it's downstairs and to the right. Most of the downstairs area then was also exposed to the fresh air and there were no great floodlighting pylons to be glimpsed. *EH 08 May 2004*

HOME PARK 1951 and plans are unveiled for the new Grandstand at Home Park. Fifty three years on and fans are once again eager for new plans to be unveiled. Note the inside of the main entrance in the distance and the corner of the old changing room block on the far left of our then picture – the small stand now occupied by the Police and Security, the Public Address studio and the Chisholm Lounge. Named after one of the Argyle stars of the 1950s one can only speculate as to who might be remembered in the naming of any new rooms as and when Phase Two sees the completion of the new Stadium. *EH 01 May 2004*

HOME PARK It is hard to hoist in the changes here at Home Park. When the final phase is complete it will be harder still to accept that the changes have all taken place around the pitch, or that this isn't a new location and that it really is Home Park turf; where visitors are still impressed at any stage of the season. Older fans will doubtless be able to recall the days when even the earlier coverings on the Lyndhurst and the Devonport End were new, and one can only really guess at the likely appearance of the stadium in another 50 years time. But then who knows what league Argyle will be in and what appetite there may be for live football? *EH*
03 May 2002

PLYMOUTH ARGYLE This was the tangled remains of the pre-war stand at Plymouth Argyle after a night-time raid by German Bombers. Ironically a large amount of furniture and pianos had been stored in the football stand area for 'safe keeping' during the Second World War as it was quite a distance from the vulnerable city centre. But the Pilgrims laid new foundations and the same scene today shows the back of the main stand at Home Park. *EH 26 Oct 1998*

NORTH ROAD STATION There have been quite a few changes to North Road Station over the last 40 years. But amazingly, if you look at the foreground and background, it is remarkable how similar it all is. Take Glen Park Garage. It has changed little from the outside, and there are still quite a few features inside that were there in the fifties. The brick pillar in the foreground gives us our key reference point, but another common denominator is the top floor of the Pennycomequick Sorting Office building – how much longer will that be there? Beyond that, we see part of Central Park, and if you look carefully you will see many more trees now than there were then. There is also less clutter on the slope behind the sorting office, as several of the allotments have long since disappeared. *EH 18 Nov 2000*

DEVONPORT PRISON Built in 1849, Devonport Prison was, at one time, deemed to be the most cost-efficient prison in England. Unfortunately, though, such a statistic was not enough to save it and in 1877, after less than 30 years service, it was closed, along with another 37 nationally as the Government attempted to streamline the Prison Service. Today only that part which housed the governors and porters of the old Borough Prison survives and there you see them in the old photograph with the entrance running right through the central tower block. Now used exclusively for residential purposes, these attractive Victorian dwellings sit between Wake Street and Holdsworth Street, opposite the sorting Office at Pennycomequick. *EH 05 May 1998*

CORPORATION ROAD For those who like to test their memories a clue to the date of this photograph is there next to the typical British workman leaning on his shovel. It's on the number plate of the lorry UFJ122J – which means that if it was brand new it would be sometime around 1970, certainly no earlier. In fact it was just a little later... 25 March 1972 the photo is dated and if memory serves, the destruction of Hermon Terrace took place over a single weekend, a real "now you see it, now you don't" affair. Today a long block wall marks the old back lane of the terrace and on the other side of it, then as now, is Corporation Road.
EH 05 May 1998

FARLEY'S FIELD Farley's Fields were used by many groups and schools locally for sporting and leisure activities and for those that used them it was generally a tantalising experience as the distinctive smell of warm, freshly-baked Farley's Rusks wafted across the open space. If the exercise didn't make you hungry that smell certainly would! Here we see Farley's Field in use in August 1952 for Scottish Country Dancing at a Country Fair. Today of course the familiar Farley's aroma has long since gone from here and now the giant supermarket chain Safeway occupies the site, the fields themselves largely given over to car parking for the store.
EH 05 May 1998

MANADON ROUNDABOUT It's hard to imagine now, but when our Then picture was taken this area had only just become a part of Plymouth. Yet today it is not far from being the geographical centre of the city. The views are just up from the Manadon roundabout; the key element in both is the Golden Hind pub, which was newly-built when the first picture was taken in the late 1930's. It was in 1938 that Plymouth won a boundary extension that meant an instant city growth from 5,711 acres to 9,595 acres. When the first picture was taken, the Royal Navy was only a year or two away from occupying the large Manadon estate on the hill in the distance. Now that occupation has come to an end, and one by one traces of the Naval presence are being eroded. Little changed in the centuries leading up to the one now about to close, this area has changed greatly over the past 60 years. A few older trees help give us our bearings as does the road itself, despite being much widened. We can but wonder on the lifespan of the flyover, what will this scene look like in another 60 years? *EH 19 June 1999*

MANNAMEAD ROAD The road is much wider and this scene, which is Now right in the middle of city was Then right on the northern extremity. Taken just a couple of years before the beginning of the last war, our Then image shows us the approach to Mannamead Road. Hartley Service Station is just behind the trees and a little beyond the bend in the road on the left in our Now picture, but back Then there was much less traffic on the road, especially here, more than forty years before the construction of the Manadon flyover. *EH 1999*

SWEB OFFICES In February 1972 when our Then picture was taken, the offices of the South Western Electricity Board in Outland Road, were brand new. The Manadon Roundabout that we know today was still some years off and the take over of SWEB even further into the future. Back then there was a petrol station just out of view to our right, now this busy road does not lend itself to anymore stop-start points than is absolutely necessary. Not surprisingly there have been changes to the surrounding planting, however the building shows few signs to indicate the passing of more than thirty years. *EH 26 Mar 2005*

CROWNHILL SHOPS 1971-2001, thirty years separates the two images and yet apart from the changes in car design, and in the style of keep-left bollards, the main stretch of Crownhill shopping centre looks much the same as it has done for a long time. Although when you look again, you can see a number of differences; to our right the expanded Co-op has undergone a major, and not altogether sympathetic, transformation, the Lloyds Bank frontage has been revamped and further down, towards the main Tavistock Road, the garage has gone. Essentially however the by-passing of this stretch in the late 1960s has eased the pressure for change to the basic layout, in much the same way as the by-passing of the Ridgeway did at Plympton a few years later. *EH 10 Feb 2001*

CROWNHILL VILLAGE The road passing through the village was the main road Then, and while it no longer fulfils that function, it is nevertheless a great deal busier than it was when horse power relating to a wheeled carriage meant simply the number of horses pulling that carriage. The distinctive, late-Victorian, Tamar Hotel was new back Then – note the railings at the front, so common a feature around Plymouth before the war. Back Then, of course, this was well outside the Plymouth boundary, and would remain so for a few years yet. It was, in fact, part of the St Budeaux parish, but it was relatively self-sufficient as a village in its own right. *EH 12 Nov 2005*

CROWNHILL FORT It was the construction of the main Palmerston Fort, a mile or two outside Plymouth, on the site of two cottages at Knackersnowle that ultimately brought about the change of the name of the village there. The cottages that were destroyed had been known as Crown Hill as indeed they sat on the crown of the hill. As the only one of the Plymouth forts to be properly equipped and manned this great structure – recently restored – was a great boost to the local economy and so it was logical enough that the name of the barracks, as it was then home to a greater number of people than the village, came to be substituted for the old name of the community. As the years passed so other military developments sprang up in the area. Today, however, they have all disappeared and Crownhill is a busy and heavily-populated part of Plymouth. The roads here have been greatly expanded to cope with modern demands, but the Fort entrance can just be seen in both pictures, peeping out from between the trees on the skyline. *EH 24 Mar 2001*

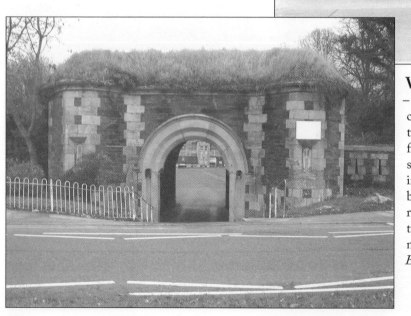

WOODLAND FORT If only walls could talk – and I know there's some people who think that they can and do – what stories would this gateway have to tell. Little could the men who built Woodland fort and those who worked on the other twenty or so surrounding the Three Towns back in the 1860s, have imagined that almost 150 years on and this is would be more or less the middle of modern Plymouth rather than an outpost a few miles north of the old town. Incidentally, apart from the road markings not a lot of change here over the last few decades! *EH 13 Dec 2003*

CROWNHILL How long ago do you think it was that the road was being built in the main picture? 1967 it was begun, 1968 it was completed and yet now its hard to remember just how it all looked before. Long gone are the Plumer Barrack buildings, although a few of the long single-storey premises remain and behind the TC Rolt, Mercedes garage, it is just possible to make out the Masonic Lodge at the end of Smallack Drive and beyond it Charlton Road. On the left of the pictures Crownhill Fort, now open to the public, is hidden behind the trees, while behind the bushes to the far left is Crownhill Police Station. *EH 05 May 1998*

CROWNHILL POLICE STATION Taken from the last-but-one storey of Crownhill fire station training tower, the key linking these two pictures is the pattern of the paths and roads. The large area to the left of the foreground is now a car park, and across the road – Budshead Way – from it is now Crownhill Police Station. On the other side of Tavistock Road, where Plumer Barracks and the Garrison Church still were in this 1971 picture, we now have the Land Registry Buildings. In the distance, on the far right, Crownhill Village is little changed from this angle, although we have a much clearer view of Crownhill Methodist Church, which now sports an extension at the front. *EH 05 May 1998*

HONICKNOWLE RECREATION HALL Graham Langston it was who provided this deceptively simple Then & Now pairing in which we see Honicknowle Recreation and Reading Hall as it is today and as it was in 1934 when the extension (with the three windows) had just been built. The hut dates originally from 1912 and for the first thirteen years of its existence it stood around the corner from Butt Park Road, behind the Methodist Church. The re-opening, after the extension, in August 1934, preceded the celebrated, crowd-pulling Honicknowle Week. MP Mark Patrick opened the new extension, famous local boxer Len Harvey had hoped to make it, but telegrammed his apologies for being held up. Still a key part of Honicknowle life, the 'Rec', which hosts bingo, line dancing, healing and other activities, was given a marvellous make over by Owen James over the last few months, and is currently 'looking as good as it ever has done'. *EH 25 Mar 2006*

HONICKNOWLE It's perhaps not easy to make it out but there is a clump of trees on the skyline of both pictures that is among the most obvious links between the two views. Visible from all directions, the trees are near the junction of Byron Avenue and St. Peter's Road, Honicknowle, and we are looking from Budshead Road today, although the older picture, which shows the beginning of the Whitleigh Estate in 1949, was probably taken from a little further up in what is now Lancaster Gardens. The trees by the lorry are quite likely those to the left our Now picture. Note the houses of Old Woodland Road in the middle distance. *EH 05 May 1998*

WIDEY LANE

Widey Lane, looking south, in 1968; the skyline is much the same, the houses are at the top of Linketty Lane (East) and to the right many of the original trees can still be seen. Widey Court School, opened in 1963 but not actually completed until the following year, is off to our right, on the edge of Widey Woods. Once a very rural and somewhat muddy and pitted backwater, this is now quite a busy bus route. *EH 05 May 1998*

WIDEY LANE Heralded as the "School of the Future," Widey Technical School opened in September 1959 and here we see it, just visible between the trees in 1968. At this point in time the builders were widening and extending Widey Lane which formerly ended just beyond here, where it met Linketty Lane. Now, of course, Culver Way takes the route right round to Eggbuckland, much of it running just yards to the north of the Parkway. In 1972 Widey Tech became Widey High and in 1988 the school was closed and the site redeveloped for the red-brick houses that occupy the grounds today. *EH 05 May 1998*

DRAX GDNS Look carefully at the old view of Drax Gardens and you can just see, at the top of the new road that is being created on the mound, the fence that is in the foreground of this view. Today, apart from trying to pick out the same trees 30 years on, we can verify our location from the pavement and low wall in the foreground to the right of both pictures. Here we stand today looking across the bottom of Widey Woods, the Parkway just down from the little roundabout now created here. *EH 05 May 1998*

EGGBUCKLAND Before the 1930s Eggbuckland was very much an isolated village on the edge of Plymouth and even, as you can see, in 1964, the area around the church still had that village flavour. But one by one the fields around were being developed and here in the middle distance of our old picture we see the first houses of the new Eggbuckland estate – on Downside, Dale, Moorfield and Orchard Avenues. Note the post-war prefabs at the end of Orchard Avenue, very popular with many of their occupants, these cosy little places with their built-in fridges were quite a novelty in their day. Donnington Drive occupies the foreground today and elsewhere the spread of "new" housing can be seen filling up the fields, although clearly there are one or two still untouched today. *EH 05 May 1998*

THE COMPTON INN The exact date of our Then picture is unknown, but we can safely assume that the best part of a century separates these two images of the Compton Inn and while there have been many changes to what was then lovely little rural village a mile or two outside of Plymouth, there is still plenty that is recognisable. The pub itself has extended into the shop next door, and the roof line has been raised, at the end of the terrace, however, the property appears much as it did, and beyond that, behind the trees, there is still a delightful Georgian house. Further into the village another erstwhile shop has gone, but the building remains, while on the far right of our Then image we see the corner of what was Compton School, before it relocated up the hill some forty years ago. Doubtless the man on the steps with his sleeves rolled up was the Then landlord of the Compton, Robert Moule who also ran the grocery here for twenty years, just as the couple leaning on the wall in our Now shot are the current licensees – Dave and Chris Brown - although they retire next week after nineteen years. *EH 08 Oct 2005*

COMPTON SERVICE STATION There was a time when garages sold petrol, and if you were lucky, oil, wiper blades, batteries and a few other car-related bits and bobs. The date on the back of our Then picture is 18 September 1956 – almost half a century ago. The price on the pumps ranged from 4/1d to 4/7d a gallon (that's around 20p to 23p a gallon or around 5p a litre). Today it is almost twenty times that … what will it be in another fifty years? Will there even be any petrol left? Wind the clocks back a hundred years and there was no garage, but probably a blacksmith ready to shoe your horse if you had one, somewhere close at hand, so who knows what the future holds. In the meantime we all need food for survival and increasingly we seem to need to be able to park very close to the shop we're using otherwise we might struggle to carry everything, hence the number of shops that have sprung up on and around filling station sites, like this one here in Compton, just off Eggbuckland Road. *EH 29 Nov 2005*

EMMANUEL CHURCH Emmanuel Church was built in three phases and it was always intended that there should have been a fourth, which would have completed the structure with a spire – indeed there is a drawing inside the front entrance, showing how the completed building was to have appeared. Here we see it in our Then picture just after the initial phase had been finished, which it was in 1870. Note the lack of development all around, save for what appears to be the house known as Hollybank at the top of the rise to the right. In 1887 a second corner stone was laid for the construction of the transepts, chancel and vestry and in 1895 a third foundation stone marked the commencement of work on the tower. *EH 24 Dec 2005*

THORN PARK On the face of it, it's difficult to date the older image. Clearly a timber specialist looking at a cross section of one of the impressive trees today might be able to give an approximate age for them and then subtract whatever age he or she thinks they may have been in the earlier snap, but there is a handy clue on the other side of our old postcard of Thorn Park – it was posted in July 1905 and as we're looking at an autumnal scene it must be at least 100 years old! No cars then in the approach to Mutley House – that's the gate at the end of the road and note how the wall on the right has grown too, the original height still observable by close examination of the structure today. *EH 19 Feb 2005*

PLYMOUTH COLLEGE It's a view that's very familiar to those who know Ford Park, College View or Devon Terrace and although a fall of snow can often create a sense of timelessness, the lads in our snowbound scene were out on the playing field of Plymouth College more than seventy years ago. Although we have no specific date we can see the science labs to the left that were completed in 1927, while to the right we can see the then unfinished end of the main school building. Only ever a part of the original scheme this block, opened in 1880, was not completed until 1934 when windows were created in this wall and a gymnasium, with classrooms above, were created at the back. Note incidentally the pre-war gable roof end of Hyde Park School in the background (it was rebuilt, flat, after incendiary damage during the war). *EH 10 Dec 2005*

FORD PARK LANE A two-way thoroughfare with houses fronting the eastern side of the street – that was Ford Park Lane fifty years ago. Ford Park Villas then Ford Park Cottages, were the two subsections seen here on our right, these properties in turn backing on to the back of Mutley Plain itself. At the northern end can be seen the distinctive Barton Motor Company building. Built in 1930 on the site of a residence once known as Cleve Villa, the Barton Building played a significant part in Plymouth's motor trade for forty years. Although still standing, it has long since been divided up into smaller units, while major parts of the rest of the lane have been cleared – in many cases to help the viability of the shops and commercial premises they backed on to. *EH 13 May 2006*

FORD PARK Television was newly arrived in town and renting a set was the favourite option of many as the two vans parked alongside the Empire Snooker Club here bear witness. We're looking down the eastern end of Ford Park Road towards Mutley Plain. Officially there's no parking in this stretch now, but fifty years ago, when there were fewer cars around, there was parking – and there were no traffic lights controlling the flow of traffic onto the Plain. Long gone now is the snooker club, and that stretch now houses part of Sommerfield's supermarket on the corner here. On the other side of the road, Perilla's Fish and Chip shop has long since occupied what was, half a century ago, Joseph Dingle & Son's Mutley branch of their butcher's business. *EH 20 May 2006*

MUTLEY PLAIN Two Views a generation apart, but what is the main difference between them? It's the number of signs, fences and kerbstones that have been put in place to control traffic flow, for vehicles and pedestrians. Once pedestrians crossed the Plain at will and there was no need for traffic lights: there was hardly any traffic. But as this has increased, so has the need to try to keep pedestrians safe. It is interesting to note that while most of the businesses have changed, the large lamp-posts illuminating the Plain are just as they were. *EH 10 May 2000*

MUTLEY PLAIN Several generations grew up around the Mutley area of Plymouth familiar with Charles Harding's furniture store. It occupied a handful of neighbouring properties between Belgrave Road and Connaught Avenue. Our Then picture, from 1973, shows the shop in its later years. It closed in the 1980's and is occupied by Blockbuster Express Video store and Threshers Off Licence. This end of Mutley Plain has yet to experience the sort of increase in licensed premises that the southern end has had in recent years. But the oldest hostelry on the strip, the Hyde Park Hotel, continues to do good business. Probably the most significant change since 1973 has been the controversial addition of the Mutley toilets. With the help of some tasteful cosmetic work, planting and painting, the toilets seem to have been better received – even if they are not always open. *EH 27 May 2000*

CONNAUGHT AVENUE It is quite amazing how much more open Connaught Avenue, and indeed many other Plymouth thoroughfares, looked before the advent of the motorcar. Admittedly the trees have also grown substantially and also have a view-restricting impact on the scene. But now try to imagine the street without a single car and you may realise that this view and many others like it have actually lost very little of their original Victorian grandeur. Appropriately, the street was named after Queen Victoria's son, Prince Arthur, the Duke of Connaught. Connaught (or Connacht) is the north-western province of the Republic of Ireland and includes Sligo, Mayo, Roscommon, Leitrim and Galway (and the famous Galway bay). *EH 12 Feb 2000*

MUTLEY PLAIN "Plymouth's leading shopping centre 46/47" is how the old picture is captioned and that is how it was just after the war. Mutley Plain was largely spared from the devastation that befell the City Centre and in the immediate post-blitz period Dingles had several shops there, they occupied both of what are now the Ingleside and Carlton homes. Carlton was the children's outfitters, "tops to teens and inbetweens", and a whole generation of schoolchildren were kitted out there. John Yeo were in the building now occupied by Summerfields; there was a big Boots there and a Timothy Whites. A busy commercial centre it was but clearly the photographer managed to catch it when it was quiet, although it would be difficult these days to find a time when it looked anything like that quiet. More cars, more traffic generally and fewer trees today, and fewer opportunities to cross the road wherever you wanted to. Note also the loss of the big Methodist Church – much missed particularly at Christmas when there seemed always to be a splendid nativity scene outside at the top of the steps. *EH 18 Dec 1999*

MUTLEY PLAIN Lunn Poly, Alan Power, Wheelers, Pengelly's – whatever the name above the door, the building on the corner of Mutley Plain and Ford Park Road has long been a prominent premises. The addition in recent years of more traffic lights has ensured motorists who regularly use this route have had an opportunity to take stock of the changes. From the first floor up, those changes have been minimal – the 'upper' aspect of the Plain has changed little in a century. But the ground floor, and even the street and pavement layout, gives us a more interesting account over the last 20 years. Many traditional shops in our Then picture from 1980 have gone, replaced by offices, fast food outlets and licensed premises – though these changes are more apparent on the eastern side than the part of the western side we see here. *EH 09 Sep 2000*

38310. MUTLEY PLAIN, PLYMOUTH.

MUTLEY BAPTIST CHURCH More than half a century separates the two images and yet there's little obvious difference in the surrounding buildings. There are a number of changes here though and they all have to do with the motor car. For not only are the cars the most striking indicators of the passage of time but also the measures taken to accommodate that particular means of transport account for: first, there's the removal of the trees from the other side of the road, including outside Mutley Baptist Church – which formerly had a much more pedestrian friendly frontage. Second, note the introduction of traffic lights to slow the traffic and allow pedestrians to cross. And third, there's the erection of railings along the length of the Plain to stop pedestrians crossing at will - as they used to. Note also that while the tram lines have long since gone, public transport (from a distance) has changed in design much less than private transport - see the similar shape of the double-decker buses at the end of the Plain in both pictures.
EH 20 Nov 1999

MUTLEY PLAIN It's hard to imagine that the time will come when a future generation will look at the Now picture and think to themselves 'wouldn't it be nice to still have buses like that on the road today'. But some people looking at these pictures now are doubtless hankering after the golden age of the tram. Apart from the road surface, traffic and road signs, the main difference between these two long-separated images is not in the buildings – which are little changed externally – but in the planting. Mutley Plain, as we can see, was once charmingly tree-lined, and what a subtle improvement it makes, softening the hard, angular lines of various properties along its length. *EH 27 Jan 2001*

MUTLEY PLAIN Structurally there is little difference in the external appearance of the buildings in these two pictures. Although 20 years separate the two, had we gone back before the war the changes would still not be all that marked. But internally the changes here in the past decade have been quite radical, and most reflect the impact of the expansion of the University of Plymouth. The Nottingham pub expanded into the next door premises and became the Freebooter and Firkin. Then the Lipton building, which became Lexerten, was converted to a Hogshead pub. Next came Bar Italia (and the Cavern), Café Sol and Boomerangs Sports Bar, resulting in five licensed premises where previously there were none. Throughout this period, the U Wash laundrette still trades under the same sign, while Insurance brokers Denmans, opticians Leonard Gibson and the Co-op remain. *EH 19 Aug 2000*

MUTLEY PLAIN A Then, Then and Now here, with two of the images from opposite ends of the same century (*top and bottom*) and what a contrast they make. Curiously enough the bricks, glass and mortar structures are much the same, with the notable exceptions of the post-war rebuild on the end of Alexandra Road and the removal of Mutley Methodist Church in the late 1970s, but the appearance of traffic using Mutley Plain and the pedestrians traversing it, has greatly changed. Quite what the early Edwardians would have made of their late Elizabethan descendants we can only guess for even those whose lives span a century have to adapt their attitudes as life moves on. The sheer volume of motorised transport on the road, the complete absence of horses from the town and lack of clothes covering the arms and legs would surely have come as a shock to most of those captured in the oldest picture were we able to pluck them out of the one picture and place them into the other. *EH 09 Dec 2000*

FREEDOM FIELDS Doubtless Doreen Mole's Then picture is an image that many can still conjure up in their mind's eye, indeed anyone familiar with that scene who hasn't been back there in the last few years may be surprised at the changes, for they have been great. The last patients left Freedom Fields in February 1998 and soon afterwards the site was sold and cleared, only the Grade II Freedom House just outside the entrance to Freedom Fields Park in Greenbank Terrace, was left standing. A private housing estate rose up on the site and the street names were chosen to commemorate the nurses killed at the hospital during the war. *EH 15 Jan 2005*

BOWYERS For more than a century, this distinctive red-brick chimney was a major landmark on the last leg of the railway journey into Plymouth's North Road Station. It was a prominent feature from many angles, including the busy Alexandria Road on to which it fronted. Built as the New Bedford Brewery sometime in the 1880s, it became the Beechwood Factory after the brewery moved out in 1921 and Brown, Wills and Nicholson became the new owners. After a few more changes in the late 1950s, it became Bowyers at the dawn of the 1960s and remained theirs until they moved out to Plympton. On May 15, 1980, the towering chimney came down, and before long the old buildings were gone and new, less visually-interesting warehouses sprang up on the site. From this angle, those buildings are now screened by buildings and vegetation. *EH 16 Dec 2000*

ST AUGUSTINE'S An interesting Then and Now here as we see St Augustine's in Alexandria Road prior to being bombed and then the post-war rebuild. Sadly, the church has been closed for some time now and its future is uncertain. Time was, however, when it was a busy and popular church. Carved out of the parish of Charles in 1904, it was damaged in the Blitz of April 1941 and almost completely destroyed in a subsequent bombing raid. When newly built, it stood alongside the Bedford Brewery, which later became the Beechwood Factory and then Bowyers before it was demolished in 1980. Already there have been a variety of neighbours on the adjacent site and currently Eurobell have their Plymouth base there. (nb: the church has since been demolished)
EH 25 Mar 2000

LIPSON HILL An early publication, which featured our Then photograph, had an interesting caption to go with it. It read: "Before the building of the Laira Embankment and the making of Embankment Road 100 years ago, all the vehicular traffic into the town from Ridgway and Ivybridge had to traverse the very steep Lipson Hill. "A few years ago, although just a mile from Plymouth, this area had quite a rural appearance, but now enterprising builders have crowded the hill with houses."That caption was written the best part of 100 years ago. Back then, Mostyn Avenue had yet to be built and Lipson Vale ran right up to the bend in the road as it curves around the hill. Now Lipson Vale refers just to that part linking Alexandra Road and Old Laira Road, and the short stretch running up from it to Lipson Hill Road has been long since re-christened Savery Terrace. *EH 02 Dec 1999*

ROSEBERRY AVE On the western corner of Rosebery Avenue and Salisbury Road you will find Salisbury Road Baptist Church, a rare local example of a bombed church outside of the city centre being rebuilt on its original site. Would the corporal in the right of the picture have realised the church would be rebuilt? Nearly 60 years on and, for the houses of Rosebery Avenue, it looks pretty much as though time has stood still, from the outside at least. *EH 05 May 1998*

SEYMOUR AVENUE This house in Seymour Avenue, near the junction with Beaumont Road, St Judes, has been rebuilt since it was blitzed during the last world war. The Blitz picture shows the front of the building completely blown out - and yet the houses either side of it seem virtually untouched! And a young schoolboy kicks his heels as workmen shovel the rubble under a still precariously positioned roof. There's no date on this old photograph, but Plymouth's last raid wasn't until April 1944. Today the avenue looks as good as new. *EH 24 June 2000*

BEAUMONT ROAD The walls, the church (now largely obscured by trees), the kerbstones and even the railings are all still here today to give us our bearings as we look along two images of Beaumont Road, separated by over a century. Back then, a single lamp was set in the middle of the junction with Tothill Avenue, its raised base providing a seat for the weary pedestrian. Impossible to imagine today as the traffic flow here is controlled by four sets of sequenced lights. What will this scene look like in another 100 years? It would have been hard to imagine in 1892, when this view was taken, that the relatively recently-built railway would not last longer than it did. But many have happy memories of Friary Station where now we find houses and superstores and, more specifically to this view, the Friary House Doctor's Surgery. *EH 24 June 2000*

BEAUMONT PARK The absence of people, advertisements or signs, and the minimal intrusion of the motor car render these two views more alike than the passing of over 100 years would suggest. The best indication of the passage of time is the girth of the tree in the foreground, as each season adds another wooden ring to its waistline. Otherwise there is little change. The old Beaumont Park lodge has had a few coats of paint over the years and the houses at the bottom of Tothill Avenue have been well looked after. And, although you can't really see it for the foliage, St Jude's Church appears today much as it did then. *EH 05 Feb 2000*

145

EMBANKMENT GARAGES Thanks to Trevor Lear for this wonderful seventies shot of the two garages that sat either side of the A374, on the approach to Marsh Mills, before the widening of the Embankment. Many will recall the old road prior to the creation of extra lanes inbound and outbound, following the infilling of the little tidal creek on the edge of the Plym. The Shell signs here are now consigned to the memory bank and old photo albums - with one garage grassed over (in front of the extended white house) and the other buried beneath the road - there is now a Texaco garage just visible behind the three-chevron slow-down warning, roughly where the old Crabtree Inn was. Note also the three outbound British Austin motorcars - a reminder that not only was the road different then, but so was the type of traffic on it! *EH 30 Sep 2006*

UNDERWOOD ROAD Underwood Road in Plympton is one of most narrow and ancient routes in the area. Parts of it are little changed from the late 19th or early 20th Century, as these pictures show. Indeed parts of it date back much further than that. The pub, from the outside at least, has changed very little. The hanging sign at the front has been replaced by a larger sign at the side, but the bracket for it is still there, above the entrance. The high wall on this side of the pub gone, but the general vista, including the chimney pots, is remarkably unchanged. One wonders what the men outside the pub would have thought had they seen a car like the one in our Now picture. *EH 15 Jan 2000*

ELBURTON HOTEL When Vincent Hart, who supplied these two images, lived in Elburton, in the late 1950s, there was petrol station 'owned by the Kents who also ran a taxi service' to the left of the picture at the junction with Springfield Road. He adds, "immediately on the left as you entered what is now all Springfield Road, the ten semi-detached houses were called 'Doreena Villas' where my wife and I lived.' The Then picture Vincent believes to date from around 1950 and he points out the ladies from what would appear to be a local bowling team, standing outside the Elburton, itself little changed in half a century. Note, however, the roadside fencing and that while the houses on the right of the road are also little changed the other side of the road has become almost all road with the dualling of the carriage way into Plymouth. *EH 22 April 2006*

HOOE Thanks to Robin Blythe-Lord of Hooe for this splendid pair of images; "I would estimate that the then postcard was photographed sometime around 1960/61 because the white building showing just above the roof of the school on the right is the Infants building which was finished in 1960 and there appear to be iron railings around the school and these were removed in August 1961. The infill at the end of the lake was started in 1963. The building with the awning to the right was then Steven's butchers' shop (now a private house) and to the right of that was the Mountbatten Social Club which was demolished in 1997/8." *EH 24 July 2004*

MOUNT BATTEN It was rescued back in 1962 thanks to the actions of the Old Plymouth Society, at a time when it had been proposed that the tower should be demolished because it was unsafe. Clearly the extensive quarrying of this part of the Mount Batten headland had left the 17th century tower (it is contemporary with the Citadel) in a precarious position. Happily however the situation was favourably resolved and now that the site has become open to the public again – it was part of the RAF base in 1962 – many can now enjoy the fine views from around the tower and headland itself. *EH 07 May 2002*

MOUNT BATTEN More than a hundred years separates these two images and what a lot of changes this headland has witnessed in that time. For a good 20 years or so after our Then picture was taken it was business as usual for the little bit of boat building and boat repair work carried out here. People from Plymouth were ferried across from the Barbican by the local watermen and walked from here around to Jennycliff and beyond. Then, in 1913 Mount Batten became a flying base and for the next eighty years or so that is how it remained, off limits to most civilians. Now once again open to the public, the old RAF buildings have mostly disappeared and a new, accessible, era has opened up - the one constant feature however, the 17th century tower, a contemporary of the Royal Citadel, is still its most prominent landmark. *EH 19 May 2001*

MOUNT BATTEN Thanks to Peter Carlyle for this pair of photos, I believe Peter took both images, one just a few weeks ago, the other back in 1967. At that time the ancient headland was still very much in operation as an RAF base, and while many traces of that era have been eradicated, there are still plenty of reminders. But whatever the recent history of this site it always worth remembering that in the hundreds, thousands, of years before air travel, and before sea travel even, this was a prime location for local inhabitants. With its narrow isthmus, Mount Batten was relatively easy to defend and it is no great surprise to find that most of our earliest, local, man-made artefacts have been found here. *EH 08 Jan 2005*